Wir
Airfare Game

Save Money and Stress on Every Flight

Charles McCool

Winning the Airfare Game

Save Money and Stress on Every Flight

by Charles McCool

Hawk Ridge Press
P.O. Box 2755
Reston, VA 20195-0755
www.HawkRidgePress.com

ISBN: 0-9705119-2-2
Library of Congress Catalog Card Number: 00-192600
First Paperback Edition 2001
Printed in the United States of America

Winning the Airfare Game may be purchased in bulk at quantity discounts for fundraising, promotions, or other purposes. Customized books or book excerpts can also be created to fit specific needs. For information, please write: Hawk Ridge Press, Special Sales, P. O. Box 2755, Reston, VA, 20195-0755.

Printed in the United States by Morris Publishing
3212 East Highway 30 • Kearney, NE 68847 • 1-800-650-7888

Acknowledgments

Sincere appreciation is extended to all that contributed to *Winning the Airfare Game,*

particularly:

Carol, Janie, and Rachel in California
Susan in Connecticut
Joanne in Florida
Bill and Mary in Massachusetts
Laura in Ohio
Celeste and Jane in Virginia

and for providing inspiration:

Les Brown
Arthur Frommer
Suzanne Hogsett
Dan Poynter
Rick Steves

Last, but by no means least, eternal gratitude to Julie for everything.

Contents

This book is dedicated with love to Julie and the twins

Preface

My fascination with getting lower airfares peaked in the early 1990s when I was able and fortunate enough to fly (from California) to South Korea, Hong Kong, Hawaii, Australia, Florida, and Europe. The total cost for the flights would have typically been more than $2,500, but I paid nothing. In fact, I paid less than nothing, since I received money from the airline.

Most likely, I would not get the same results today. I was in the right place at the right time, asked the right questions, and reaped the rewards. What I learned from these—and numerous other—flights contributed to the topics and strategies in this book. Incidentally, the Story following Chapter 6 explains how I was paid to take those flights.

About Airfares

Since the mid-1990s, two independent business practices have revolutionized the air travel industry.

First, the Internet has permeated the public mainstream as a new and viable source for buying air travel tickets. Consumers can book airfares using the same reservation system that travel agents use. The airlines have been quick to adopt the Internet and encourage consumers to use it, as it is their least expensive distribution source.

Second, commissions paid by airlines to travel agents have been reduced several times. Many travel agencies are closing or merging into huge conglomerates. Even more important, almost all travel agencies have shifted their focus from booking air travel to selling tour packages and cruises; service fees are charged for previously free services, including booking air reservations.

One result of these two ongoing activities is the creation and development of the book-it-yourself process. Until the early to middle 1990s, travelers had to buy tickets from a travel agent or the airline. Being able to find your own airfare and book your own ticket is extremely appealing to many consumers.

Finding the lowest airfare is not an easy task. You hear about a great fare, check the Internet or call the airline or a travel agent, and discover that the fare is not available. On the flight, you discover that another passenger paid 50 percent less than you did. It is easy to become frustrated trying to get lower airfares.

Buying tickets is particularly frustrating because airfares constantly change. According to an article in *THE WASHINGTONIAN* magazine, there are over 100,000 fare changes daily, with various fares for each flight. Most passengers on any given flight pay different prices, even though the seats are identical. Many factors determine the cost of airfares, including—but not limited to—what airline is flown, where and when you fly, who you buy from, when you buy, and who you are.

In order to get the lowest airfare, you must usually buy your ticket more than two weeks before the flight. Airlines charge a fee to make changes to a ticketed itinerary. This is different from almost every other industry. Imagine paying for your birthday meal at least a month in advance. On your birthday, you cannot select a different meal, eat at a different time or place, or change the people that dine with you. It does not matter if you are out of town, not hungry, or no longer like the people you selected a month earlier.

Unusual, also compared to other industries, is the refund policy of airlines. If an airfare drops after you buy a ticket, the airline is reluctant to give you money back. A department store, on the other hand, will issue a refund (upon request) if an item goes on sale within 30 days.

Because of the Internet—and the media touting its benefits—many consumers believe that they can easily find the lowest airfare on their own. Buying air travel has become a book-it-yourself phenomenon. However, airlines have a very complex pricing structure and most consumers are justifiably confused, especially because travel agents no longer offer free advice. This book presents topics and strategies to assure that you will get the lowest possible airfare for every flight.

About This Book

Around 1990, I started collecting information for this book by flying as much as I could. Since every person and situation is unique, there can be no magic formula for saving money on *every* flight. However, I determined that three primary factors existed for getting the lowest possible airfare in most situations. I call them the **Principles of Getting Lower Airfares**: being flexible, resourceful, and assertive.

Figure 1
McCool Rule: Principles of Getting Lower Airfares

- Be Flexible
- Be Resourceful
- Be Assertive

Nearly everyone can benefit from *Winning the Airfare Game.*

- Independent book-it-yourself travelers can learn and use strategies throughout the book to get lower airfares.

- Families, students, seniors, and others will discover appropriate and valuable discounts and programs (see Chapter 2).

- Package travelers will learn how to enhance their tours with add-on fares and frequent flyer programs (see Chapter 3).

When a fare quote is higher than expected, changing the day or time of a flight, the airport or route, or even the airline usually decreases the airfare. **Chapter 1** explains how being flexible results in lower airfares.

Sometimes, lower airfares depend on "who you are" or "who you know" instead of "what you know." **Chapter 2** outlines many discounts available to travelers based on who they are. The chapter also describes and analyzes many sources that sell air tickets.

Expanding on the basics of lower airfares from the first chapter, **Chapter 3** explains how being resourceful can result in lower airfares. Topics include alternative air travel scenarios—such as co-terminals and open jaw flights—and resources, including last-minute airfares and frequent flyer programs.

Asking for a lower airfare often works! Sometimes, consumers must be assertive and explicitly ask about the lower airfare strategies in **Chapter 4**; agents may not be familiar with the topic or are reluctant to tell you.

Problems can occur while trying to get, or after getting, lower airfares. **Chapter 5** describes how to avoid risky situations and unscrupulous vendors, keep low airfares, enjoy flights, and handle problem situations.

The best time to learn about getting lower airfares is before you need to buy a ticket. Then, when you must fly somewhere, you will be familiar with appropriate strategies and resources. **Chapter 6** describes resources that can help you get lower airfares, including the Internet.

The **Appendix** section is extensive. It includes the following sources for getting lower airfares:

- dozens of addresses and telephone numbers
- over 250 Web sites
- a bibliography of helpful books and magazines

Using the principles, strategies, and resources in this book as a guide, anyone can get lower airfares for their next (and EVERY) trip. Good luck!

About the Author

Charles McCool has traveled—always on a tight budget while trying nearly every cost-cutting approach—to more than two dozen countries on five continents and 49 of the United States. He has helped countless people save money, stress, and time on their trips, and has written many articles about getting lower airfares and other economical travel topics. Mr. McCool has lived in several areas with alternate airports, including South Florida, Southern California, Northern California, and Northern Virginia, where he currently resides. He has used America Online since 1991 and the Internet since 1994.

Comments or questions about this book, requests for information, and ideas for future projects can be sent by:

Mail: Hawk Ridge Press
P. O. Box 2755
Reston, Virginia 20195-0755

WWW: < LowerAirfares.com >

E-mail: Charles@LowerAirfares.com

All feedback is welcome. If you find this book valuable, please recommend it to family, friends, co-workers, librarians, bookstores, Internet newsgroups, and others. If not, please let me know why, along with your suggestions for making subsequent editions better. I enjoy hearing from readers and learning how the book helped get lower airfares. Thank you!

Hawk Ridge Press will pay for submissions that are used in its publications. They accept stories, tips, and strategies about effective economical travel—including getting lower rates for rental car, lodging, cruises, travel packages, extended travel, luxury travel. Current needs, payment policies, and guidelines are listed at its Web site < HawkRidgePress.com > and available from the above address; send your request along with a self-addressed, stamped envelope.

1

Opening Moves

Learn the basic rules of the airfare game. This chapter provides the information to enable you to make most simple reservations. To get the lowest airfares, be as **flexible** as possible when planning trips. Varying the day, time, airport, or airline usually results in a lower airfare. People flying only on a certain airline, in First Class, or on specific days pay higher airfares.

Most examples in this chapter use a fictitious family, the Tripps. The Tripps are two adults and two children, ages 10 and 15, shopping for a flight from New York City—Kennedy airport is closest to their house—to Los Angeles. They prefer to leave on the third Saturday in June—the day after the

end of the school year—and return on the fourth Sunday in June.

Buy Early

The lowest airfares must be bought 14 or more days before the flight departs. Airlines reward early buyers with discounted airfares—also called APEX[1], excursion, or supersaver fares—while penalizing last-minute travelers with the highest fares. For example, a 14-day discount fare for a flight between Boston and San Jose, California costs $355 while the same flight bought less than 14 days before flying costs $938. Even last-minute airfares, which are becoming increasingly popular, rarely cost less than 14-day APEX fares.

If you cannot buy a ticket 14 days prior to flying, you may get other discounted fares seven and three days before the departure date. New York-to-Chicago flights cost $230 two weeks before the flight, $400 seven days prior, and $1,000 three days prior. Los Angeles-to-San Francisco flights cost $81 when bought seven or more days in advance but $240 three days before the flight.

Although seats can be reserved 360 days in advance, there is no additional discount for buying more than 30 days before the flight. However, it is best to buy tickets as early as possible because the number of discounted seats is limited. After selling all the seats in each fare class[2], the airline sells subsequent seats in the next, more expensive, fare class; no matter how many days it is before the departure date. Once ticketed, an airfare price will not

---

[1] **APEX** – advance purchase excursion.

[2] **Fare class** - a group of seats with qualifying requirements. An example is K14NR, meaning K class, 14-day advance purchase, non-refundable.

increase, even if the published fare rises. One can request a travel credit or refund if the price drops.

In exchange for lower fares, airlines restrict discounted tickets in several ways; they are non-refundable, non-transferable, and must be paid for within 24 hours of the initial reservation. Other restrictions include staying at your destination for a Saturday night, returning within 30 days, making no interim stops, and flying specific routes[1]. The dates, days, and times of travel are limited and usually must be during off-peak periods (see **Seasons of Travel** in this chapter).

Be very certain about your travel plans before buying discounted tickets. Passengers making date and routing changes to discounted tickets must pay a $75 fee, plus the difference between the ticketed and current airfare. The change fee usually dissuades passengers from buying advanced purchase tickets and then changing flight dates and times.

> **The Tripps are flying on a popular route at a busy time of the year and should buy their tickets long before the departure date. As the following table shows, the 21-day and 14-day fares are the lowest:**

---

[1] **Route** – the airports used for a trip. Kennedy-to-LAX is a different route than Newark-to-LAX. New York-to-Los Angeles is not a route because specific airports are not named. Although not technically correct, a city name is often used when there is only one airport; for example, Boston-to-Baltimore is formally Logan-to-BWI or Logan-to-Baltimore.

Figure 1.1
McCool Jewel: Sample APEX Airfares

Days before Departure	Major Airlines[1]	Discount Airlines[2]
21	$516	$317
14	$516	$367
7	$1,186	$448
3	$1,844	$448

If all 21-day and 14-day fares were already sold, the least the Tripps could pay is $448 (on a discount airline) or over $1,100 on a major airline—even if they buy their tickets more than 21 days before the departure date.

Fare War

The lowest airfares are offered during **fare wars**. A fare war is a sale by all or several airlines for particular routes or regions. When airfares for the entire system are on sale, it is called a **system-wide fare war**. Fare wars usually begin with one airline reducing airfares, followed by other airlines matching or exceeding the initial sale prices.

Fare war prices are usually lower than discounted rates. They typically have additional restrictions along with penalties for changes or cancellation. Restrictions include

---

[1] **Major airlines** – the largest non-discount US airlines, which are American Airlines, Continental Airlines, Delta Air Lines, Northwest Airlines, Trans World Airlines, United Airlines, and US Airways.

[2] **Discount airlines** – low-frill or no-frill airlines offering lower airfares than major airlines. They include America West Airlines, Midwest Express, and Southwest Airlines.

dates, days, and times of travel, length of stay, and advance purchase.

Fare wars may start and end at any time. Traditionally, though, airfare sales occur each year:

- Between late May and early June
- In late August
- Between Thanksgiving and Christmas

There are several ways to know that a fare war is in progress. Use a good travel agent and be one of the customers that they notify. Travel agents constantly look up fares on the computer and are the first to know when a fare war breaks out. Listen to radio and television shows for news about fare war sales. Sign up for e-mail notifications from airlines and travel Web sites. Many Internet sites, like the My Yahoo (< Yahoo.com >) portal, display current fares for selected routes. A sudden price change for several routes is a good indication that there is a fare war sale.

Fare war prices can apply to less popular routes and smaller airports, even though newspaper ads will only list major routes. Call your travel agent or the airline and ask if fare war prices are available for your desired route. For example, several ads listed $84 fares for flights between Boston and Washington, DC (Dulles airport). Lower prices—$98 and $118 instead of $250—were also available for flights between Manchester, NH and Dulles.

Although the Tripps are flying in late June, they should pay attention to fare wars, which may occur before Christmas, six months before the flight.

Routing

Varying the airports used for a trip (**route**) can result in a lower airfare. Each route—also called **city pair**—has a unique set of airfares that differ from all other routes, including other airports in the same city. For example, Newark-to-Miami fares are different from Kennedy-to-Miami fares.

Competitive routes served by several airlines have lower fares, while routes served by a single carrier are much more expensive. For instance, the Cleveland-to-Boston route is dominated by Continental Airlines. Cleveland-to-Boston flights cost 50 percent more than competitive routes of similar length, such as Cleveland-to-Atlanta.

It is important to realize that direct flights are different than non-stop flights. **Non-stop flights** travel directly between the departure and destination airports without stopping. **Direct flights** make one or more stops but passengers do not change planes. **Connecting flights** require passengers to change planes in an interim airport. If you are told that a flight is direct, ask if it is a non-stop or connecting flight.

Most people prefer non-stop flights because the travel time and the chance of a problem—missed connection, weather delay, or mechanical breakdown—is less. Some travelers, particularly families, break long routes into shorter flights, creating the opportunity to stretch in connecting cities.

Figure 1.2
McCool Jewel: International Connecting Flights

When forced to make a connection for a returning international flight, save time by doing so outside the United States.

For example, a flight from Frankfurt, Germany to San Francisco connects in Washington, DC or London. Passengers connecting in Washington must clear Customs there, check in for the flight to San Francisco, and then retrieve their baggage in San Francisco. Passengers connecting in London will clear Customs in San Francisco, eliminating the baggage transfer hassle.

There is no consistent rule about which type of flight costs less. An airline may charge more for a non-stop flight because it is convenient. Then again, for certain routes, the non-stop flight might cost less than the connecting flight. For example, early flights through Denver's new airport cost $40 more, because of an airport surcharge; a Boston-to-San Francisco flight connecting in Denver was $40 higher than the non-stop flight.

Many airlines use a **hub and spoke system**. Flights go through a common airport or **hub**, where passengers change planes, or **make a connection**, for the second flight. For example, Delta has hubs in Atlanta and Salt Lake City. Delta flights between Dallas and New York are likely to connect in Atlanta.

The Tripps are flying on a popular route served by many airlines. They should be able to find good fares for a non-stop flight. A connecting flight may be less expensive, especially if there is no fare war when they buy their tickets.

Saturday Night Stay

By waiting until Sunday or later to take the return flight, you will likely get a lower airfare. In fact, almost all discounted airfares require passengers to meet a **Saturday night stay** restriction.

> **A flight leaving Boston on Monday and returning from San Jose, California the following Friday costs $710, even when purchased more than three weeks before flying. The same flight returning on Sunday, two days later, costs $355. Dulles-to-Los Angeles flights meeting the Saturday night restriction cost $275, while flights that do not cost $1,300.**

Some travelers stay extra days in order to get lower airfares. In the above Dulles-to-Los Angeles example, returning on Sunday instead of Friday will save you $1,025 ($1,300 - $275)—the saving is more than the additional two day's expenses. Other travelers circumvent the Saturday night stay restriction with **back-to-back** tickets (see Chapter 4).

Many fares on discount airlines, and some on major airlines, do not require a Saturday night stay. For instance, on competitive routes, major airlines remove the Saturday night stay restriction to match discount airlines rules.

> **The Tripps will qualify for all discounted fares because they will be at their destination for a Saturday night.**

Discount Airlines

The presence of a **discount airline**, such as Southwest Airlines, at an airport means lower airfares from all airlines. Major airlines must reduce prices on routes that discount airlines serve in order to remain competitive. For instance, Baltimore has lower fares for many routes because of Southwest's presence. Flights from Baltimore to Salt Lake City are $204 compared with $360 from the other two major airports in the area—Dulles and National—that do not have discount airlines for that route.

Fares are much higher on major airlines than on discount airlines. A *New York Times* article showed that for flights over 1,500 miles, Southwest charges six cents per mile and the top three major airlines charge nine to 11 cents per mile. The average Los Angeles-to-Chicago fare was $210 on discount airlines and $473 on major airlines.

Discount airlines offer lower airfares because they eliminate or reduce some aspects of the air travel process. Some no-frill and low-frill tactics include serving simple snacks or no food, issuing tickets at the airport, and offering only non-assigned, "first-come first-served" seating. Some discount airlines do not sell tickets through travel agents; passengers must call the airlines. Many discount airlines do not have frequent flyer programs.

Many travelers will not fly on discount airlines because of these concessions. Other passengers use discount airlines whenever possible because the savings outweigh the inconvenience. It is a personal choice.

Consider yourself fortunate if a discount airline serves a nearby airport. Even if you do not use a discount airline, the fares from all airlines are lower because of the discount airline's presence.

The Tripps might spend less money on a discount, rather than major, airline flight. The lowest fare of $417 on a discount carrier, connects in Chicago (only on the westbound flight). The lowest fare on major carriers was $531 (from Newark airport) or $554 (from Kennedy airport); both carriers offered non-stop flights. The Tripps can determine

whether the lower price is worth the inconvenience of a connection.

Seasons of Travel

You will get lower airfares by not flying when demand is highest, during the **peak season** or **high season**. Airfares are 25 to 50 percent lower during the **off-peak season** or **low season**. The off-peak season varies by destination, but fares are generally lowest for flights from mid-January to March and from October to mid-December (except Thanksgiving weekend).

Some destinations, including Europe and Hawaii, have a three-tiered pricing structure—or three seasons: peak, off-peak, and shoulder. The **shoulder season** is a period when the number of visitors is tapering off but not at the low point of off-peak season. A shoulder season bridges the gap between peak and off-peak seasons.

Some destinations have more than one peak season. For most Caribbean destinations, the peak travel periods include the winter months and June (honeymoon month). Peak periods for Hawaii are mid-December to mid-January, mid-February (President's weekend), and the week after graduation.

Peak seasons for most destinations are usually, but not always, based on good weather. Fares to South Florida are highest from November to April, coinciding with the best weather. On the other hand, Orlando's peak season is during the summer, when school is out and more families can visit Disney and other attractions. This is also the period of the worst (hottest and wettest) weather.

You can get lower off-season airfares to many popular tourist destinations without sacrificing decent weather. Check the typical off-season weather patterns for your desired destination before buying a ticket. For example, Hawaii has good weather all year; the average temperature in the summer is only seven degrees higher than in the winter. The ideal time to visit Hawaii is when the prices are lowest and the tourists are relatively scarce—March, April, or mid-September through mid-December.

The peak season for California includes the summer, when schools are not in session. The Tripps will be flying during peak time. Peak season airfares are usually more than $400 but can be as low as $250 during fare wars. Low season fares between New York and Southern California can be as low as $198.

Day of Week

Airfares to most destinations are lowest for flights between noon on Tuesday and noon on Thursday. Flights on Friday, Sunday, and Monday are usually the most expensive. Depending on the routing, Saturday flights can cost the most or least, but are usually somewhere between.

When a fare quote is higher than expected, ask if any flight within a day or two—before or after—has a lower fare. Request the lowest fare within a date range. For example, request the lowest fare for flights leaving the 10th through the 14th. A preferred flight may have no seats at the lowest fare but flights on other days might.

Sometimes you can get a lower airfare by extending your trip for a couple of days. Instead of returning on Sunday, you can probably get a lower fare on Tuesday. On the other hand, by changing your return flight from Thursday to Saturday the airfare may only increase $10, but you can stay an extra two days. It is a low-cost strategy for maximizing the value of your travel.

Synchronizing air travel and lodging components can be a challenge. Many properties or destinations require that guests arrive and depart on a specific day of the week, such as Saturday. The days for a low airfare may not match those for the lowest lodging rates. For example, a hotel may charge $150 Sunday through Thursday nights and $75 for Friday and Saturday stays. The lowest airfare is for travel on Thursday, while Friday flights cost $70 more. It may require some effort and research, but your goal should be get the lowest overall travel rate without sacrificing the quality of the trip.

The third Saturday in June is extremely popular for New York-to-Los Angeles flights, so the lowest fares will sell far in advance. Flights leaving Newark on Thursday and returning on Monday are $125 less than flights from Saturday to Sunday ($430 vs. $305). Even leaving a day earlier, Friday instead of Saturday, will save the Tripps $50 per ticket ($380 vs. $430). They should consider flying on other days, instead of their current Saturday to the next Sunday plan, to get lower airfares.

Time of Day

You can get lower airfares by flying at certain times of the day. Flights during non-peak travel times—before 7:00 A.M., after 7:00 P.M., and 10:00 A.M. to 3:00 P.M.—usually cost less than flights during "rush hour."

Even if fares are the same throughout the day, the availability of the lowest fares might vary. When getting a higher than expected fare quote, ask if there is a lower fare on a flight leaving earlier or later the same day. One flight may have no seats at the lowest fare while a flight at a different time will have cheap seats. Ask agents[1] to check around until you get the lowest possible fare.

On flights between Ft. Lauderdale, FL and Washington, DC you can save $30 by leaving at 11:30 A.M. ($154) instead of 3:00 P.M. ($184). When flying one-way between Los Angeles and Salt Lake City on Delta, the 6:30 A.M. flight is $89 and all others are over $220.

> **Between New York and Los Angeles, airfares generally do not change based on the time of day. In other words, the lowest priced seats are available on all flights. However, midday flights are more popular and their lowest priced seats would sell more quickly. It would not be unusual for airfares to be higher for an 11:00 A.M. flight than a 7:30 A.M. flight; simply because all of the lowest priced seats for the 11:00 A.M. flight have already been sold. The Tripps can fly at any time, so they should be able to get the lowest available fare.**

Alternate Airports

You may be able to get lower airfares by using **alternate airports** rather than the most common or popular ones. For instance, flights to Salt Lake City are $150 lower from Baltimore than from Dulles or National airports (see also **Discount Airlines** in this chapter).

New York, Chicago, and several other metropolitan areas have more than one airport. There are five airports within 40 miles of Los Angeles—LAX (Los Angeles International),

---

[1] **Agents** refer to anyone that makes air travel reservations, including travel agents, airline's reservation agents, Internet booking engines, and other sources. See **Chapter 2** for a complete discussion of Agents.

Long Beach, Burbank, Ontario, and Orange County—and many others within two hours—including Bakersfield, Palm Springs, San Luis Obispo, Santa Barbara, San Diego, and Ventura. There are three major airports within 30 miles of Washington, DC (National, Dulles, and Baltimore) and several smaller ones within a three-hour drive, including Norfolk, Philadelphia, Richmond, and Wilmington.

For each trip, determine which airports (departure and arrival) are a reasonable distance and ask agents to specifically check fares to and from them. Agents usually have a predetermined list of alternate airports. For instance, most agents consider Fort Lauderdale to be the only alternate airport for Miami. You should also consider West Palm Beach, Fort Myers, Tampa, Orlando, or Key West—if the trip includes them—as alternate airports for Miami.

There is an Internet source that shows the closest airports to anywhere. This example uses Beverly Hills, California:

- **Go to < Travelocity.com >**
- **Select "Search for the closest airport"**
- **Enter "Beverly Hills" for City**
- **Select "California" for State**
- **Click Go**

Results include commercial and non-commercial airports:

Airport	Miles
Los Angeles	9
Burbank	9
Long Beach	23
Orange County	41

Ontario	**46**
Oxnard/Ventura	**47**
Norton Air Force Base	**67**
Santa Barbara	**86**
Carlsbad	**92**
Bakersfield	**101**

Only you can decide if the additional time that is needed to reach an alternate airport is worth the potential saving. For example, flights from Chicago to Louisville are $100 less than to Cincinnati but an additional 75-minute drive each way is required.

It takes practice to determine the best alternate airports. To ensure that agents are checking fares from all possible airports, ask questions like, "Is there a lower fare to (or from) any airport within 100 miles of {your departure city}?" Travel agents and Internet sources are more likely to provide such information, since airlines only search their own fares.

Flights to smaller airports may cost less, because discount airlines are more likely to fly there instead of major airports. Even if you cannot get lower airfares, you will save time and aggravation when flying into smaller airports. At smaller airports, baggage claim, car rental, and ticketing functions are much easier to navigate, and traffic is lighter. When fares and routing are reasonably similar, consider flights into smaller airports, such as Oakland or San Jose instead of San Francisco, Burbank instead of Los Angeles, and Fort Lauderdale instead of Miami.

The Tripps can select from several departure and arrival airports. Any Los Angeles area airport would be acceptable and there are also several airports within an hour of their home (LaGuardia, Kennedy, Newark, Islip, and Westchester County). The lowest fare from each New York area airport is

to LAX. The lowest fare from Newark is generally $100 less than from Kennedy and $150 less than from LaGuardia. The lowest airfare is usually for Newark-to-LAX flights. Flying between Kennedy and LAX is more convenient for the Tripps but not worth an additional $400 ($100 more for four people).

Number of Airlines

Airfares are usually lowest when the same airline is used for an entire trip. Flying on different airlines for portions of a trip could save you money, however. Four scenarios appear below. Use a travel agent or the Internet to arrange a trip with more than one carrier; airlines will not tell you that a competitor has a lower fare and it is time-consuming to do this research.

Example 1 – Multiple Segments (Circle Trip)

A trip with more than two segments is one situation to consider using more than one airline. When flying multiple segments, also called a circle trip, rather than a round-trip, the fare will be the sum of the one-way fares. To get the lowest overall fare, select the least expensive flight for each segment, even if it means a different airline for each flight.

For a circle trip between San Francisco, Las Vegas, and Los Angeles, no major airline has non-stop flights for each leg. At the time, my preferred airline had San Francisco-to-Las Vegas and Los Angeles-to-San Francisco flights but not a Las Vegas-to-Los Angeles flight. A second airline had to be used. Even if my preferred airline did have Las Vegas-to-Los Angeles flights, it is worth checking other airlines for a lower fare. A discount airline offered Las Vegas-to-Los Angeles but not San Francisco-to-Las

Vegas flights. The result was to book the first and third segments with my preferred airline and the second leg with the discount carrier.

Example 2 – Forced Connection

It often costs less to use different airlines when a connection or stopover must be made. This situation occurs when there are no non-stop flights and only one carrier offers connecting flights. An example is flying between two small markets—such as Huntsville, Alabama to Monterey, California—where each airport has several airlines but only one airline serves both.

The single carrier for the example route forces passengers to connect in Dallas. Although several airlines offer Huntsville-to-Dallas flights or Dallas-to-Monterey flights, only one airline has both. However, using different airlines for Huntsville-to-Dallas and Dallas-to-Monterey flights results in a much lower fare. To get the lowest fare, compare the single carrier's fare to the total of the lowest prices for each segment. That is, find the lowest Huntsville-to-Dallas fare and the lowest Dallas-to-Monterey fare, add them, and compare the total to the single carrier's price.

Another example is presented in **Split Tickets** in Chapter 4. The only airline flying between San Jose, California and Cabo San Lucas, Mexico charged $600. By flying on different airlines, one can pay $300.

Example 3 – Monopolized Routes

When one airline has the only non-stop flight for a route, it charges exorbitantly high fares. For instance, the average fare for non-stop Cleveland-to-Boston flights, operated by only one airline, is 50% higher than similar length competitive non-stop flights, such as Cleveland-to-Atlanta.

Using different airlines and connecting in an interim city results in lower airfares for such routes. Instead of taking a non-stop Cleveland-to-Boston flight save money by flying through Philadelphia or even Chicago. Fly Cleveland-to-Philadelphia on one airline and Philadelphia-to-Boston on another. Other cities, including Baltimore, Cincinnati, and Washington, DC, can be used for connecting flights. The disadvantage is the inconvenience of taking connecting flights on separate airlines instead of a non-stop flight. Individual preference will determine if this inconvenience is worth the cost saving.

Example 4 – Competitive Routes

The last scenario where different airlines can be used to get a lower fare is a competitive route with reasonable one-way fares. For example, Los Angeles-to-San Francisco flights cost $100 with one-way fares of $50. Many flights are available each day on several airlines resulting in great choices.

When the lowest airfare is unavailable, select flights from different airlines until you have the lowest total fare. Assume one airline says that the lowest fare is $175 because the return flight has sold all of the lowest fare seats. In other words, the Los Angeles-to-San Francisco portion costs $50 but the return flight costs $125. Check with another airline and discover that they have $50 seats for the return flight. Book a one-way Los Angeles-to-San Francisco flight with the first airline and a one-way San Francisco-to-Los

Angeles flight on the other. The total fare is $100 and you save $75.

For routes with competitive one-way fares, select flights based on convenient departure and arrival times (see also **Co-Terminals** in Chapter 3). Even when one carrier quotes the lowest round-trip airfare, check if another carrier has more convenient flights (in either direction). Since there is no discount for booking both flights with the same carrier, select the best itinerary for you. It may be unusual to use two carriers for a simple round-trip but it is not against any regulations. See also **One-Way Flights** in Chapter 3.

Charter Flights

Charter flights sometimes have lower airfares to popular tourist destinations, including Hawaii, Las Vegas, Europe, Mexico, and the Caribbean. Charter operators—which can be travel agents, airlines, or tour operators—lease entire airplanes and sell tickets directly to the public or through agents. Flights may be a one-time event or periodic, like twice a week or every other Wednesday.

Charter flights operate from most major U.S. and Canadian cities. Sun Country Airlines offers $399 non-stop charter flights from Minneapolis to Aruba, as an example. The lowest commercial airfare for this route is $1,052 and no other airline flies non-stop. Charter flight prices are not always lower than discounted fares on other airlines. Before buying a charter ticket, check for lower airfares with other sources.

Some charter flights have benefits that commercial flights do not. SunTrips—one of the largest charter operators—offers last-minute specials, one-way fares, and package deals. Sun Country flies between Minneapolis and

Washington, DC and charges $238 until two days before the flight. The lowest discounted fare on commercial airlines, $250, is only available 14 days or more before the flight.

Advertisements for charter flights appear in travel magazines, Travel sections of major newspapers—like *The New York Times*—and other sources. SunTrips has a toll-free telephone number (800-786-8747) and Web site (< SunTrips.com >), but encourages customers to book charter flights through travel agents.

Charter flights are somewhat riskier than commercial flights because the contract is with the tour operator rather than the airline. If the charter company or tour operator goes out of business, then passengers have little or no recourse for getting refunds.

Other potential disadvantages of charter flights can include no reserved seating, smaller seats, inconsistent service, and checking in two or more hours prior to departure (longer for international flights). Charter flight prices can increase up to 10 percent before the flight and passengers are obligated to pay the additional fee. Charter flights can be delayed up to 48 hours before the tour operator is required to provide alternate transportation.

Tour operators can cancel charter flights up to 10 days before the scheduled departure, for any reason, and simply refund the passengers money. This usually occurs when too few seats are sold. However, a passenger that cancels or changes an itinerary must pay a huge penalty fee or potentially lose the money already paid.

Understand all the restrictions and rules before buying any charter flight. When an agent gives a quote for an unfamiliar airline, ask whether it includes a charter flight. Consider a charter flight when the saving is great or when it is a part of a travel package—along with hotel, rental car, and meals. For only minimal cost savings, you should not have to assume the major risks of a charter flight.

> **The Tripps can ask their travel agent if there are New York-to-Los Angeles charter flights. They should also check *The New York Times* for ads by tour operators offering charter flights.**

Class of Service

Most domestic flights have two classes of service: **First Class** and **Coach Class** (or **Economy Class**). Most international and some domestic flights offer additional seating between First and Coach class, called **Business Class**. Together, First and Business Classes are called **Premium Class**. Airlines may have different names for any or all of these classes. Coach Class seats cost much less than Premium Class seats.

A Business Class seat costs five to ten times more than the lowest Coach Class fare. First Class can be up to fifteen times higher than the lowest fare. Passengers paying expensive Premium Class fares get better service and food, bigger seats (fully reclining sleeper chairs, sometimes), more legroom[1], and customized entertainment. Most Premium Classes offer leather seats, nicer blankets and pillows, and free drinks. Premium Class ticket holders receive additional (bonus) frequent flyer points and use special check-in lines at the airport. Premium Class fares have no restrictions or advanced purchase discounts.

Many airlines offer a complimentary upgrade to Premium Class, when available, for the price of a **full-fare** Coach Class seat. Few passengers pay full-fare prices and it is a

---

[1] **Pitch** – the distance between rows. Pitch is the air travel industry measurement for legroom.

poor choice when they do. Thus, an upgrade from full-fare to Business or First Class is not a good deal. It is a marketing ploy to entice business travelers to use their airline.

Alternatives for Premium Class seats without the normal high fares include:

Some smaller **regional airlines** sell $25 one-way First Class **upgrades**. These upgrades are usually sold only at check-in gates and redeemable on a first-come, first-served basis.

Companies selling discounted Premium Class tickets include The Corporate Flyer (800-883-5937, < FlyFirstClass.com >), Ticket Planet (800-799-8888, < TicketPlanet.com >), and 1stAir.net (716-383-4470, < 1stair.net >). Check current prices on the Web site or through the office.

Frequent flyers on major airlines can exchange certificates for an upgrade from Coach to First (or Business) Class. Some frequent flyers periodically receive complimentary upgrade certificates in the mail. Airlines also sell books of upgrade certificates. Certificates can be exchanged for a class upgrade based on seat availability. Upgrades are granted on a priority basis, with the most frequent flyers having the highest priority. Some of the biggest consumer conflicts with airlines are VFFs (**very frequent flyers**) trying to get class upgrades (see **Frequent Flyer Programs** in Chapter 3).

Frequent flyers can also redeem points for a class upgrade. This strategy is especially effective when award seats are not available. For instance, a passenger can buy a Coach Class seat and use frequent flyer points to upgrade to Business or First Class.

Another option for discounted Premium Class fares is a coupon broker. Coupon brokers buy frequent flyer awards and, in turn, sell discounted Premium Class tickets. However, most airlines consider it a violation of rules to fly with a ticket from a coupon broker. Penalties when caught using a coupon broker ticket include confiscation of the ticket, termination of frequent flyer account, or payment for true cost of the Premium Class ticket. Some coupon brokers are listed in **Appendix F.**

Class of service is not a factor for the Tripps. For New York-to-Los Angeles flights, a First Class seat costs $4,200 while the average discounted Coach Class seat costs $450. The family is not considering First Class seats.

2

Know the Players

Players in the airfare game include consumers and ticket suppliers. Suppliers offer different airfares, so it is important to know how they play the game. Your player characteristics are essential to getting the lowest possible airfares. Student, senior, or group status, along with coupons and other discounts, can further reduce low fares found by applying the Opening Moves from Chapter 1.

Discount Certificates

Discount certificates come in various forms:

- **Dollar Off** certificates lower the cost of airfares, similar to grocery coupons; an example is $25 off any airfare over $250. Dollar Off certificates usually offer discounts no more than 10 percent, such as $35 off fares over $350. Certificates with bigger percentage discounts are usually for higher airfares, such as $75 off fares over $600.

- **Free Companion** and **Companion Discount** certificates permit a person accompanying a paying passenger to fly at no or little cost. Also called Discounted Rate certificates, these discounts can be used by family members or, sometimes, any two people flying together. Usually, the initial ticket costs more than the lowest possible fare but the pair costs less than two discounted APEX tickets. An example is "Friends Fly Free," a popular Southwest Airlines promotion.

  Depending on the offer, the companion and the paying passenger must have the same last name or address. In other words, the companion must be a spouse or family member, rather than a friend.

  Occasionally, airlines distribute certificates for free or reduced companion flights. An example is a free companion flight certificate when signing up for an airline's credit card. Another example is a $99 companion flight coupon given as a promotion to transatlantic flight passengers.

  One of the most valuable travel discounts, in monetary value, is a free companion ticket when buying an international Premium Class (see **Class of Service** in Chapter 1) ticket with an American Express Platinum card. Many, but not all, major international airlines participate in this outstanding program. As of September 2000, the International Airline Program had 14 international airline partners. Example flights could include Los Angeles-to-Sydney on Air New Zealand or New York-to-Geneva on Air France. Unlike most offers, this one does not require the companion to be a spouse or family member. One traveler, however, must have an American Express Platinum card

- **Future Travel Vouchers** use a "fly now, save later" approach. An example is 25 percent off the passenger's next cross-country flight after taking an airline's introductory transatlantic flight.

- **Percentage Off** certificates usually offer five or 10 percent discounts off any fare. These certificates are not as common as the other discounts.

- **Quantity Discount** certificates allow greater savings as more people fly together. For example, each ticket costs $250 for one person, $225 for two, $200 for three or four people, or $175 for five or more. They are usually for specific routes or zones.

- **Tier Discount** certificates offer dollars off savings that depend on the price of the ticket. An example is $25 off airfares between $150 and $300, $50 off fares between $301 to $450, or $75 off fares over $500.

- **Zone Discount** certificates offer special fares for travel within certain areas. As an example, Zone 1 includes states east of the Mississippi River and Zone 2 includes the western states. Flights within Zone 1 cost $99, within Zone 2 cost $159, and between the zones cost $199.

Discount certificates come from various sources, including travel agents, retail stores, and the mail.

- Dollar Off certificates may appear in magazines or newspapers.

- Airlines place Tier Discount and Zone Discount certificates in magazines.

- Retail chains offer discount certificates as a promotion, like $100 off airfares with a $50 purchase or special zone fares with $200 in grocery receipts.

- Banks offer Free Companion or other certificates as an incentive to open a new account or apply for a loan.

- Discount certificates appear in mass mailings or with frequent flyer and credit card statements.

- Percentage Off travel cards are available to convention attendees and members of travel clubs, such as Entertainment Publications.

Newspaper ads, frequent flyer newsletters, and magazines sometimes promote offers with a code number instead of an actual certificate. To get the appropriate discount, travelers must mention the code number when making a reservation.

Airlines sometimes accept competitor's certificates and discounts. Let an airline know you prefer to fly with them but will buy another airline's lower fare. Many times, the airline will find a way to accept the certificate rather than lose your business to the other airline. You may have to try a couple of times or ask a supervisor. If you do not get the desired outcome after a few attempts, thank the agents and book the other airline's fare.

Using travel discount certificates should be simple, like redeeming coupons at the grocery store. Unfortunately, the process is much more complicated. It is not unusual for the ticketing process to take an extra five minutes when using a discount certificate. Very knowledgeable agents (from the airline or travel agency) take less time to complete the transaction but still have to go through many additional steps.

Avoid this hassle by leaving your coupon and itinerary with your travel agent. Pick up your ticket later, making sure that the price and itinerary are correct. If your agent is remote, see if you can send coupons to them in advance and have them apply the discounts to your reservations. Almost all travel agencies charge a service fee (usually $5 or $10) to book an air reservation with a coupon.

In addition to using discount certificates, passengers can often apply other discounts to airfares. For instance, discounts available to seniors, families, and groups are described in other topics in this chapter.

Some examples of using discount certificates:

> **The MacArthur family (2 adults, 2 children) used a Quantity Discount certificate to reduce their total cost for a San Francisco-to-Boston flight. The lowest total airfare without the certificate was $2,000. With the certificate, they reduced the cost to $1,400, saving 30 percent. They had to connect through a hub airport in each direction but decided the $600 saving was worth the additional inconvenience.**
>
> **A couple saved over $5,000 on a Business Class flight between San Francisco and Sydney, Australia with the American Express Platinum card International Airline Program. To get the free flight, they had to fly from Los Angeles instead of San Francisco. Separate San Francisco-to-Los Angeles flights cost less than $100 each.**
>
> **One major U.S. airline offered a free domestic flight to passengers completing a transatlantic flight. This promotion was to introduce the carrier's New York-to-London flights.**
>
> **A Northern California travel agency chain distributed Dollar Off coupons through newspapers. The**

coupons allowed discounts of $25 on $250 airfares, $35 on $350 airfares, or $50 on $500 airfares.

Almost every airline credit card offers Free Companion or Dollar Off certificates when you enroll.

A grocery chain sold reduced airfare certificates to customers with $200 in receipts. Each certificate cost $10 and could be redeemed for a $199 summer cross-country flight. This was a good deal because typical summer airfares are much higher.

Seniors

Seniors travelers are eligible for discounts that can further reduce already low fares. Follow the topics in **Chapter 1** to get the lowest possible airfare and then have a senior discount applied to it. Restrictions and eligibility vary by airline, but usually passengers 62 years or older receive a 10 percent discount on most fares. Often, a senior discount must be requested, because airlines and travel agents may not automatically offer it.

Senior coupon books can also reduce air travel costs. Coupons are usually better deals for cross-country and other long flights. For more details, see **Air Passes and Coupon Books** in Chapter 3.

Most airlines give a senior discount to anyone under 62 flying with seniors. Seniors traveling with a younger spouse or grandchild can also get a senior discount for them. Companions can also buy senior coupon books but can only use them when flying with a senior.

In addition to senior airfare discounts, Continental Airlines has two programs for seniors. One is an entire year of travel for $2,000. The other program is called the Continental Freedom Flight Club; its costs $75 for the domestic club and $125 for the international version. Club members receive a 20 percent discount on flights taken Monday through Thursday or on Saturday, and 15 percent off Friday and Saturday flights. American Airlines operates the AActive American Travel Club (800-421-5600, < AA-AATC.com >); it costs $45 per year or $75 for two travelers. Other airlines may offer similar or different senior programs.

AARP members can sometimes get lower airfares than typical senior fares. For example, Virgin Atlantic Airways offers AARP members a 15 to 20 percent discount while other airlines only offer a 10 percent senior discount. Membership in AARP is $8 per year and benefits (travel and non-travel) are numerous; for instance, hotel and vacation package deals are much more abundant than airfare discounts.

Figure 2.1
McCool Jewel: International Travel News Magazine

International Travel News (ITN) is an independent magazine for high-frequency international travelers. Many, if not most, ITN readers are seniors, based on the submitted articles. Countless tips for international trips, including money-saving suggestions, appear in each issue. ITN is a no-nonsense alternative to the glossy, pretentious travel magazines. ITN will send a free issue to anyone who asks. Contact information appears below and in **Appendix H**.

Compare senior discounts and fares from various airlines to get the best deal. **Appendix A** lists contact information for the ten largest U.S. airlines. Other airlines are listed in **Appendix B**.

In addition to airlines, contact the following organizations for senior air travel discounts and tips:

Organization	Telephone	Website
AARP	(800) 842-4777	< AARP.org >
Elderhostel	(877) 426-8056	< Elderhostel.org >
Grand Circle Travel	(800) 248-3737	< GCT.com >
Int'l Travel News	(800) 486-4968	< IntlTravelNews.com >
Saga Holidays	(800) 343-0273	< SagaHolidays.com >
Smarter Living		< SmarterLiving.com/senior >

Groups (Status Fares)

Any organization—company, family, alumni, or other group—can negotiate discounted airfares for its members. Group discounts are typically five or 10 percent off excursion fares or 15 percent off full-fare rates. A specific event, like a conference or trade show, can also negotiate group airfares, also called **status fares**.

When planning a family or group trip, try to negotiate free or discounted airfares. An airline usually offers a discount to each passenger or a free ticket for a certain number of paying passengers. For example, for more than 10 people flying together, everyone can get a 10 percent discount or every tenth passenger flies free. Contact several airlines and negotiate the best possible deal. After choosing the best group discount, you can be creative about recruiting other travelers. For instance, you can offer an "early bird" discount for registering by a specific date.

Most airlines have a separate department for group reservations. Call the airline's main reservation telephone number and ask for its group travel desk; it will likely have a different name. For instance, United Airlines has a Specialized Meeting Reservation Center, whose direct telephone number is (800) 521-4041.

Check other airfare discounts because negotiated group fares are not necessarily the best deal. For example, a certificate for $50 off a $300 fare means a bigger discount and lower airfare than a group discount of $15 (five percent of $300) or $30 (10 percent of $300). For fares over $500, the 10 percent group discount is a better deal than the $50 certificate. If the certificate can be used with the group rate, then the airfare will be even lower. Also check if a senior, student, or other discount can be applied to a group fare.

Group discounts sometimes cannot be applied to the lowest possible fares. For instance, the lowest airfare might be $250 but a group discount of 10 percent can only be used with fares over $300. A 10 percent discount on a $300 fare (net price of $270) is not a better deal than the $250 fare.

Families

Airfares for children are rarely discounted. On most flights, children are charged the same fare as adults. For international routes, some airlines offer discounted fares for children flying with a paid adult. Occasionally, airlines offer "children only" fares. Children over 12 years of age may be eligible for student discounts. See **Students and Teachers** in this chapter.

Ask for discounted children fares if booking outside the lowest available rate class. Lower overall travel costs can occur by paying more for adult tickets. For example, a family of four with two children considers two flights. One costs $250 for all passengers. The other costs $300 for adults and $150 for children under 12. The total price would be $1,00 for option one or $900 for option two.

There is no charge for children under two years that share a seat with an adult. On full flights, the parents must hold the infant. Otherwise, the infant can be placed in a nearby empty seat or the family can move to a row with extra seats. Parents must buy a separate ticket to guarantee a seat for the infant. Infant seats usually cost half the adult fare.

Quantity Discount certificates can result in lower airfares for families. See **Discount Certificates** in this chapter.

Contacts for families:

AOL keyword: family travel network
< FamilyTravelForum.com >
< FamilyTravelGuides.com >
< FamilyTravelTips.com >
< SmarterLiving.com/family >
< TravelWithKids.About.com >

Compassion and Bereavement Fares

Airfares are most expensive for flights booked at the last moment. However, most airlines have special fares for people who must fly with little notice because of the death or illness of a family member or friend.

Some airlines offer bereavement or compassion fares as a percentage discount from the full-fare or other rate. Other airlines waive the APEX restrictions so that an emergency traveler can get the lowest published rate. In either scenario, proof of death or serious illness is required to get the discounted airfare.

Rules, restrictions, and fares vary by airline. Some airlines provide compassion fares only in case of death, while others also offer them for serious illness. Most compassion fares are for specific family members, like spouses, children, parents, and siblings. Other relatives and close friends may or may not be eligible for compassion fares, depending on the airline. It is worthwhile to check the policies of several airlines and compare the fares.

Seniors and students with coupons may be able to use them for last-minute flights. If seats are available, it may be worth redeeming a frequent flyer award. See **Emergency Flights** in Chapter 4 and **Frequent Flyer Programs** in Chapter 3 for specific strategies.

Students and Teachers

Most airlines sell coupon books or offer special fares to students. To qualify for student discounts, passengers must usually be under 22 or 26; proof of age and student status are usually required. Airlines occasionally have promotional fares specifically for students. Such fares are short-lived and travelers must respond quickly. Always compare student discounts with other discounted fares to get the lowest possible airfare. Learn about an airline's offerings for students by visiting its Web site or calling the reservation telephone number; both are listed, for the ten largest U.S. airlines in **Appendix A** and for other airlines in **Appendix B**.

United Airlines offers 10,000 frequent flyer points to graduating members of its College Plus program (< CollegeTravelNetwork.com > or < MileagePlus.com >). Council Travel—the travel arm of CIEE (Council on International Educational Exchange < CIEE.org >)—is the largest organization specializing in student and teacher travel. In addition to selling discounted domestic and foreign airfares, Council Travel assists with lodging, transportation, and other travel matters. They are particularly knowledgeable about hostels and rail passes. There are dozens of Council Travel offices in the United States and worldwide.

Students and teachers can use "identity cards" to get reduced airfares, insurance coverage, 24-hour assistance, and discounts worldwide. Students 12 to 25 years of age can get the International Student Identity Card (ISIC) and full-time teachers can get the International Teacher Identity Card (ITIC). An International Youth Travel Card (IYTC), also called Go25, is available to non-students under 26. All cards are issued in the United States by Council Travel and worldwide by International Student Travel Confederation (ISTC). They cost $20 and are valid for a fixed 15 month period, from September 1 until the end of the following year; e.g., September 1, 2000 to December 31, 2001.

Several companies offer teachers free travel for recruiting other people (usually teachers) for trips. A typical deal is to sign up six travelers and receive one free flight or trip. EF Educational Tours is the largest and most well known group of this type. Many airlines and travel suppliers will offer a similar deal. See **Groups (Status Fares)** in this chapter for more details.

Figure 2.2
McCool Jewel: Travel Reference Book for Teachers

For teachers, a useful book is *Travel Tips for Teachers* by Sunni Bloyd (published by Lowell House).

Contacts for students AND teachers:

Council Travel	(800) 226-8624	< CouncilTravel.com >
Educational Travel Centre	(800) 747-5551	< EdTrav.com >
ISTC		< ISTC.org >

Contacts for students:

AESU Travel	(800) 638-7640	< AESU.com >
Class Travel International	(800) 328-1509	< ClassTravelIntl.com >
Smarter Living		< SmarterLiving.com/student >
STA Travel	(800) 781-4040	< STAtravel.com >
Student Advantage Card	(800) 333-2920	< StudentAdvantage.com >
Student Travel Services	(800) 648-4849	< STStravel.com >

Contacts for teachers:

ACIS	(800) 888-2247	< ACIS.com >
American Student Travel	(800) 231-1731	< Astravel.com >
EF Educational Tours	(800) 637-8222	< EFtours.com >
Teacher's Travel Web		< TeachersTravelWeb.com >

Residents

Special discounted airfares are available for residents of certain countries, states, or cities. Proof of residency is required for these fares. Northwest Airlines, for instance, has promotions only for residents of Michigan and Minnesota. To qualify, some residents of other states rent a short-term mailbox or use a friend's address.

Residents of Hawaii receive special fares for flights between the islands. Any Hawaiian resident is eligible, even though the discounted fares are called kamaaina or "native Hawaiian" rates. Similar discounts may be available for residents of other states or countries on their native or regional airline.

Military

Military personnel and family members can fly anywhere in the world for about $25 a flight. These flights, called **space available** (or Space-A) travel or military hops, are on military aircraft that can make several stops. The planes are on official government business and unused seats are available to off-duty personnel. Many Space-A seats are listed only within 24 hours of departure.

Commercial airlines give military in uniform discounted fares. The discount varies by airline, route, seat availability, and other factors, but it is usually 50 percent. Some airlines require that off-duty military personnel fly within seven days of the start of leave or termination to receive the military discount.

Contacts for military:

< FAQs.org/faqs/military >
< Glue.umd.edu/~oard/spacea >
< MilitarySpaceATravel.com >

< MilitaryTravelGuide.com >
< USMilitary.About.com >

Clergy and Religious

Members of the clergy may receive discounted airfares. Similar to military discounts, clergy airfares vary by airline and other factors. To get the lowest airfare, identify yourself as clergy when making reservations and compare fares of various carriers. Also compare clergy fares to other discounted airfares. British Airways offers a missionary fare to passengers traveling for volunteer or religious purposes.

There are many Christian travel agencies that arrange religious trips. < ChristianNet.com > lists many Christian travel agencies, including Group Source, (800) 800-2519 < GroupSource.com >, in Nashville and Worldwide Travel, (800) 890-0445 < WorldwideTravelInc.com >, in Newport News, Virginia. Menno Travel, (800) 667-5559 < MennoTvl.com >, is a Canadian travel agency that specializes in discounted trips for clergy and religious personnel. Overseas Express, (800) 343-4873 < OVEX.com >, is a ticket consolidator that sells discounted air travel to religious and non-profit groups and individuals.

Travel Industry

A benefit for airline employees is free air travel, often in First Class. When not working, airline personnel can fly anywhere in the world, as long as they are not late for their next work assignment. Most airlines list job openings on their Web site and on an automated telephone line. Call the main reservation number and ask for the job listing phone number. **Appendix A** lists contact information for the ten largest U.S. airlines and **Appendix B** lists other airlines.

The biggest tradeoff for most free travel, also called **non-revenue travel**, is very tight restrictions. For instance, off-duty airline employees, or non-rev passengers, usually do not have reserved seats and must fly standby. They may have to select an alternate destination or wait for several flights before getting a seat. Because of the uncertainty, airline employees flying non-rev must be flexible and try not to make prior arrangements.

Family members of airline personnel sometimes fly for free. Airline employees also periodically receive Companion Certificates, allowing any person to fly for free with the employee. Occasionally the employee and companion, relative, or friend does not sit together. The employee might even be in First Class, while the companion is in Coach Class.

Travel agents and other travel industry personnel also get free or reduced airfares. Rental car company and hotel employees qualify for "industry airfares," as do airline employees get "industry rates" for lodging and car rentals. Travel agents take familiarization, or FAM, trips to learn about destinations and suppliers. The destinations and suppliers pay most of the expenses in exchange for publicity. The intent is that the agents will promote their place or product to customers. An excellent book about being a travel agent is *Part-Time Travel Agent* by Kelly Monaghan (published by The Intrepid Traveler).

There are thousands of jobs outside the travel industry with free or discounted travel benefits. All types of companies and government agencies need people to travel for business purposes.

Books that describe jobs with travel benefits include:

Careers in Travel, Tourism, and Hospitality. Eberts, Marjorie, Linda Brothers, and Ann Gisler. VGM Career Horizons.

Jobs for People Who Love to Travel. Krannich, Ron and Caryl. Impact Publications.

Opportunities in Travel Careers. Milne, Robert Scott. VGM Career Horizons.

Figure 2.3
McCool Jewel: Travel Industry Web Sites

AOL keyword: travelindustry
< AirCrewLayover.com >
< AirlinePerx.com >
< CloudBursting.com >
< CrashPads.com >
< CrewMembers.com >
< Nonrev.net >
< TTjobs.com > lists job openings in the travel industry.
Other Web sites are listed in **Appendix G**.

Who You Buy From

Travel agents and airlines sell over 95 percent of the airfares in the United States. Seventy percent of all bookings are through travel agents. Purchases made on the Internet are increasing. Less than three percent of bookings were made online in 1999 but an estimated eight will be made through the Internet in 2001. Over half of online bookings are made directly with the airlines.

Therefore, other suppliers sell a small percentage of airfares.

Sometimes the most important factor in the price of an airfare is who sells the ticket. Consolidators can offer different prices than airlines, travel agents, and even other consolidators. A discount travel agency may give a rebate. Certain travel agents have preferred supplier fares. Before buying any airfare, compare prices from various vendors.

The Big Three

Nearly all airfares are booked through travel agents, the airlines, or the Internet. Since the product is usually identical—each supplier sells the same seat and flight—consumers will buy tickets from the supplier that offers the lowest airfare. Sometimes a specific vendor must issue a ticket; frequent flyer tickets and Internet last-minute specials must be booked through the airline, for instance. As with airlines, travel suppliers can be anywhere, even across the country.

Travel Agents

Studies show that travel agents generally find lower airfares than airlines and Internet users. Travel agents are trained to find lower airfares and know how to be flexible to cut costs. A 1999 report used a walk-up (no advance purchase) Los Angeles-to-Detroit flight as an example. Travel agents found fares more than 50 percent less than the lowest Internet prices by flying to Lansing, less than one hour's drive from Detroit. Web sites, airlines, and some travel agents would not look at this alternative unless the passenger specifically asks about it. Consumers can only ask about such options when they know about them.

Travel agents save consumers lots of research time by simultaneously viewing available airfares from several airlines. Comparing prices in one list, rather than calling each airline, is easier and takes less time. By applying the principles in this book, experienced travelers can find the same airfares as travel agents, when using the Internet, or calling airlines. For example, Lansing is an Alternate Airport (see Chapter 1) for Detroit. However, travel agents may have access to airfares, not listed on the Internet or by airlines, including instant purchase airfares.

Travel agents reduce aggravation by resolving problems—such as canceled or overbooked flights—or rebooking tickets when fares drop. When problems occur, airlines are more likely to accommodate travel agent's customers than independent travelers. The travel agent can often reach a resolution with the airline after the passenger fails.

Until the late 1990s, there was no cost to use the services of a travel agent or agency. Almost all agencies now charge small fees for making changes to tickets, processing discount coupons, or planning complicated itineraries[1]. These service fees offset the decreased revenue from airline's commissions. To ensure that you are getting the best fare without taking up too much of a travel agent's time, do advance research, know your alternatives, and be flexible with your travel plans. Ask the agent for the lowest possible airfare or suggestions for reducing the price.

Make sure your current or any potential travel agent is certified. Basic travel agent certification is through the American Society of Travel Agents (ASTA). Locate any

---

[1] According to an ASTA report (published March 20, 2000 in *Travel Trade*), 88 percent of agencies have service fees and 92 percent charge consumers for using coupons or promotions.

ASTA member by calling (800) 965-ASTA or visiting < ASTAnet.com >. Every travel agency must also have an IATAN (International Airlines Travel Agent Network) number. Other organizations—such as Association of Retail Travel Agents (ARTA), Institute of Certified Travel Agents (ICTA), and National Association of Commissioned Travel Agents (NACTA)—also certify travel agents. In addition, travel agencies usually have regional certifications. ICTA assigns Certified Travel Counselor (CTC) and Certified Travel Associate (CTA) designations to travel agents passing an exam and with, respectively, five years and 18 months experience. All U.S. travel agencies must be approved by the Airline Reporting Corporation (ARC) or, in Puerto Rico and the U.S. Virgin Islands, the Agent Reporting Plan (ARP). Contact information for some travel agent organizations appear at the end of this section.

Use a travel agent that provides great service and is convenient. A travel agent does not have to be in your neighborhood. You can contact qualified travel agents anywhere in the U.S. or the world by toll-free telephone, fax, or Internet. Many agencies have toll-free telephone and fax numbers, e-mail addresses, and Web sites. Toll-free telephone numbers are particularly important in case a problem occurs during a trip. Make sure that an agent can be reached while you are traveling, when something is most likely to go wrong.

Most agencies will book any travel arrangement but concentrate on certain types. They specialize in any combination of leisure or business travel, domestic or international destinations, specific regions, types of travel (such as cruises or packages), or activity (such as Eco-travel, adventure, or family). To determine a travel agency's specialty, ask the agents or examine their store display, *Yellow Pages* ad, or Web site.

Use a travel agent specializing in your desired destination or travel activity. For instance, when booking vacation flights to Switzerland, find a travel agent that specializes in leisure travel to Europe. A travel agent with knowledge of Southern Europe or Switzerland would be even better.

Figure 2.4
McCool Rule: Selecting a Travel Agent

1. Check Certification – ASTA, IATAN, CTC
2. Match Specialization to Your Needs
3. Service – Can They Plan All Trip Components
4. Compare Fees
5. Reliability
6. Convenience – Local, Web, 24/7 Access

Even the best travel agents cannot help with every aspect of a trip. They cannot book frequent flyer tickets, apply all discounts, or reserve many bed and breakfast rooms. Most travel agents cannot book courier flights, many consolidator flights, and flights on some airlines, like Southwest Airlines. They charge fees to process discount coupons or will not accept them at all. They may not always find the best fare. You should research and find a good travel agent in advance, not when you are desperate to book a flight.

In addition to making arrangements, travel agencies are tremendous sources of information. They have or can get brochures for any destination. They can use their computers to easily compare prices from several vendors. They can provide qualified recommendations, such as specific sections of towns, hotels or restaurants, and sights to visit *and* avoid. Travel agents occasionally travel but not whenever they want. After all, they work full-time with relatively low pay. Most free and discounted travel benefits actually go to agency owners and managers.

Figure 2.5
McCool Jewel: Travel Brochures

Travel agents have or can get brochures for just about any destination. You can request brochures by visiting < Desto.com >, formerly Worldwide Brochures < WWB.com >.

Travel agents may switch agencies. If you are comfortable with a specific travel agent, then you will want to continue working with her or him at the new agency. However, if you use a different agent each time you call or visit an agency, then it will not matter if an individual agent leaves.

Your travel agent may keep a profile with data such as your seating preference, frequent traveler numbers, and credit card information. You can even save time and eliminate potential problems by faxing or e-mailing travel requests.

Some travel agencies and chains offer their own frequent buyer program. A typical award is a free round-trip flight after spending $25,000. This can be a great deal if you make travel arrangements for other people and get reimbursed. As with airline frequent flyer programs, do not sacrifice good service for the sake of accumulating points.

Contact information for travel agency organizations, consortiums, co-ops, and franchisers:

Airlines Reporting Corporation (ARC)
(703) 816-8525 < ARCcorp.com >
American Society of Travel Agents (ASTA)
(800) 965-ASTA < ASTAnet.com >
Association of Retail Travel Agents (ARTA)

(606) 269-9739 < ARTAonline.com >

Carlson Wagonlit Travel
(800) 337-2537 < CarlsonTravel.com >

Institute of Certified Travel Agents (ICTA)
(800) 542-4282 < ICTA.com >

International Airlines Travel Agent Network (IATAN)
(516) 747-4716 < IATAN.org >

National Association of Commissioned Travel Agents (NACTA)
(703) 739-6826 < NACTA.com >

Travel Savers
(800) 726-7283 < TravelSavers.com >

UNIGLOBE
(604) 718-2600 < Uniglobe.com >

Vacation.com
(800) 843-0733 < Vacation.com >

Airlines

In most industries, consumers save money by buying products directly from the manufacturer. This is not true with air travel since booking with airlines does not translate to lower prices. Buying from the airline means no commission is paid to a travel agent, but the airfare is still not lower. Over the last several years, airlines have reduced the commissions paid to travel agents, forcing most agencies to charge service fees. This has led many passengers to book directly with the airlines.

Generally, airlines offer the same products and prices as other sources—mainly travel agents and the Internet. However, certain products—such as last-minute and instant booking airfares—must be purchased directly from the airline. Also, airlines sometimes sell products, such as back-to-back and hidden city tickets, that they call "illegal" but penalize other distribution sources for selling.

While travel agents book more than 70 percent of all tickets, airlines sell over half of the tickets on the Internet. Airlines recognize this shift in consumer spending and encourage passengers to buy tickets online. In January 1999, Delta charged a fee for any ticket *not* purchased from its Web site. Expect airlines to try other experiments, since the Internet is their least expensive distribution source.

In May 2000, it was announced that United Airlines would acquire US Airways. Within a month, it was revealed that other major U.S. airlines were looking to merge or acquire each other. The United-US Airways merger will take a few years to complete. When the dust settles from the airline mergers and acquisitions, three supercarriers would remain and, many believe, airfares will steadily increase.

As long as Southwest Airlines—or any other discount airline—serves a route, the airfares offered by all airlines will remain relatively low. A new discount carrier called DC Air is slated to emerge from the merger of United and US Airways. This is potentially good news, especially for travelers using airports served by the new airline.

Appendix A lists contact information for the ten largest U.S. airlines. Other airlines are listed in **Appendix B**.

Internet

The number of book-it-yourself purchases made using the Internet is growing at an astounding rate. A Forrester Research study predicts that almost $5 billion in Internet travel purchases will be made in 2000 compared to $654 million in 1997. Two to three percent of all bookings in 1999 were made online. It is estimated that eight percent of all bookings in 2001 will be made using the Internet. Over 50 percent of online bookings in 1999 were made directly with the airlines and airlines estimate that they will make 60 percent of online bookings by 2002.

In the late 1990s, the Internet became a viable source for buying airfares. In a remarkable shift, consumers do most of the work while airlines have not reduced prices. With few variations, airfares on the Internet cost the same as from airlines or travel agents. Delta and US Airways periodically offers a five percent discount on flights to and from Florida, for instance. Instead, most Internet sites lure consumers with incentives—such as bonus frequent flyer points, rebates, and contests.

Since consumers do the work but get no price break, why do we use the Internet? Internet users have more control when searching through available fares and flights. We can spend as much time as necessary before making a decision. Using the Internet, you can look at many options and determine what is the least expensive and most convenient flight. When calling airlines or travel agents, consumers are given fare quotes only for specific routes and dates. Agents usually do not volunteer alternatives. Most consumers do not know what to ask in order to get a lower airfare, especially when agents quickly communicate fare quotes and related information.

For more information about using the Internet to get lower airfares, see the **Internet** section in Chapter 6.

Figure 2.6
McCool Jewel: Comparison of the "Big Three"

	Advantages	Disadvantages
Travel Agents	• product comparison • experience	• service fee
Airline	• instant booking fares	• no product comparison
Internet	• book-it-yourself • occasional discount	• time-consuming • fear of technology

Other Airfare Suppliers

Consolidators

Consolidator airfare prices are usually 20 to 70 percent less than airline's published rates. Consolidators buy seats from airlines at a fixed price or percentage discount and resell them to the public. Even with the consolidator's profit, consumers can get good deals. Also called **bulk** or **negotiated fares**, consolidator fares are available year-round but most useful in the summer when fares are highest. Although most consolidators sell only international tickets, some sell last-minute domestic airfares. Always compare consolidator offerings with fares from conventional and other sources.

Consolidators sell tickets to consumers, travel agents, or both. Ask your travel agent if they use consolidators for international tickets. Many travel agencies will book consolidator tickets but will not mention it unless asked. Passengers can buy tickets directly from some consolidators. Most consolidator companies that sell to consumers have names like Air Fare Busters, Cheap Tickets, or Travel Bargains and place advertisements in major newspaper's Travel sections and other publications. **Appendix F** lists contact information for some consolidators.

Most consolidator flights are on major airlines. The agent can tell you the airline when you make a reservation. Some, but not all, consolidator fares are eligible for frequent flyer points. There may be a surcharge for using a credit card or a discount for paying in cash; each is usually one to five percent. Consider paying the extra fee, because travel purchases made with credit cards are protected from fraud.

Disadvantages of consolidator tickets include limited selection, difficult and costly itinerary changes, and perhaps no frequent flyer points. Selection is limited because consolidators buy directly from airlines. Consolidators sell tickets for only one airline or, maybe, a few carriers. Also, most consolidator tickets are non-changeable. Those tickets allowing changes have fees so expensive that it is essentially better to buy a new ticket. If your travel plans are flexible and you can accept its conditions, then you might save a lot of money with a consolidator fare.

Three large and well-known consolidators—including Euram, a long-time and popular one—went bankrupt in 1998. Lessons learned include:

- **Use a credit card.** Most of the customers that used a credit card were reimbursed. Those that paid with cash or checks were not.

- **Get an actual ticket.** Some consolidators do not print and issue the ticket until about a week before departure. Most customers without tickets did not get refunds.

Although most consolidators sell only international tickets, some sell discounted domestic (and international) tickets for a major airline (TWA). The airline allows a former CEO to sell tens of millions of dollars worth of tickets at a 25 percent discount (until 2004). Most of the companies selling these tickets are consolidators but some are regular travel agencies. Ads listing "20 to 25 percent savings on a major airline" are likely from one of these companies. These discounts are not available through TWA or every travel agency. Many of the discount travel agents and consolidators listed in **Appendix F** sell these tickets.

Discount Travel Agents

Discount travel agents, also called **rebaters**, split airfare commissions with their customers. Customers can receive a rebate or save four or more percent on each purchase. The rebate or discount may be received as the transaction is processed or several weeks later, after the agency receives its commission.

Most discount travel agencies do not find flights for clients. Instead, the customer gives all the flight information to the discount travel agent and the agency issues the ticket.

Some discount travel agencies charge annual, postage, or transaction fees. Almost all have a minimum transaction amount, usually $300. **Appendix F** lists contact information for several discount travel agencies.

Tour Desks

Tour desks are affiliates or subsidiaries of airlines that sell vacation packages—various combinations of airline, lodging, rental car, dining, and entertainment segments—for popular tourist destinations. Tour desks offer lower total prices compared with separately buying each trip segment. When independently arranged, components of an $800 package may cost $500 for airfare, $600 for hotel, and $250 for car rental. You would save $550 by buying this package.

Packages are particularly good sources for last-minute travel since they do not have advance purchase or Saturday night stayover restrictions. A cross-country flight leaving in less than five days usually costs at least $1,500, while a tour desk package with five nights lodging might cost $800. Learn about available last-minute specials by calling a tour desk or travel agent, or visiting an appropriate Web site.

For more information see **Package Deals** in Chapter 3. Most airline Web sites have a link to their vacation company (tour desk) Web site.

Contact information for some tour desks:

< AAVacations.com >	(800) 321-2121
< CoolVacations.com >	(888) 346-3641
< DeltaVacations.com >	(800) 654-6559
< NWAWorldVacations.com >	(800) 800-1504
< SunTrips.com >	(800) 786-8747
< UnitedVacations.com >	(800) 377-1816
< USAirwaysVacations.com >	(800) 472-2577

Buy online or from a travel agent?

Since each supplier's product is usually identical—same seat and flight—a consumer usually buys a ticket from the supplier offering the lowest airfare. Other factors that can determine who to buy airfares from include customer service, reliability, and familiarity (brand loyalty, past experience, or friend's recommendation).

Savvy consumers will sometimes use travel agents and other times buy directly from the airlines, depending on who offers the lowest airfare. Note that when buying a ticket on the Internet, you are using either a travel agent or airline. Check every source each time, because an online travel agent, a traditional "brick and mortar" travel agent, an airline's telephone reservation system, or the airline's Web site might offer the lowest fare.

Airlines and travel agents essentially offer the same products and prices, but there have been some battles over airlines offering products that travel agents cannot. For example, airlines sell back-to-back tickets but travel agents caught selling them receive substantial penalties.

It is not always in the airline's best interest to quote the lowest airfare. They will tell you the lowest fare for the exact route and time period you specify. They will seldom volunteer that a flight at a different time, on a different day, or to another airport costs less. They certainly will not tell you that another airline offers a lower airfare. Travel agents are beneficial because they will tell you which airline offers the lowest fare.

After finding the lowest possible airfare, you can book the ticket with a travel agent or the airline. When the price is the same, using a reliable travel agent is recommended. Building and maintaining a relationship with a travel agent can pay off in many ways. For instance, they can inform you of appropriate travel deals and can resolve travel problems more effectively than most passengers.

Many travelers are equally comfortable buying tickets on the Internet, calling the airline, or using a travel agent. It depends on the situation.

Boston-to-Dulles (Washington, DC) round-trip fares can be as low as $88 with one-way tickets as low as $44. When using a certificate or applying a senior discount, the cost is even lower. Since the travel agent's commission is something like $3 to $7, they will not spend much time researching flights.

It is usually easier to book cheap tickets directly with the airline instead of a travel agent. The airline will create an e-ticket (electronic ticket) or mail the ticket to the passenger at no cost. It takes about five minutes to complete the process. Occasionally, the airline agent gives a higher than expected fare quote. In that case, ask if the $88 (or $44) fare is available for that flight. If it is not available for a specific flight, ask about earlier or later flights. This route has several flights a day, so the lowest fare is usually available on some flight.

Even if I do not book a ticket using the Internet, I will usually search online for available flights and times. When I call the airline, I know the flight number and times of departure and arrival—for alternate flights, too, if the preferred one is unavailable. I tell the airline agent that I want two tickets for flight #123 or something similar.

3

Winning Strategies

Resourceful and savvy travelers apply specific strategies to their current situation to get lower airfares. This chapter lists many strategies that, used in conjunction with the first two chapters, will help you get lower airfares and win the airfare game.

Frequent Flyer Programs

Frequent flyer programs were created to encourage passengers to continue flying on the same airline. It is worth joining several frequent flyer programs—they are free to join—just to receive their member newsletter. Frequent flyers may be eligible for lower airfares that are not available to the general public. They may also receive coupons and special offers by mail and in the newsletters.

Frequent flyer programs are similar to restaurant or retail store programs where consumers buy a certain number of products and get one for free. Five cross-country round-trip flights, roughly, earn enough points for one free domestic U.S. flight—25,000 points are needed in most programs. Some programs offer multiple awards at a discount, such as two domestic tickets for 40,000 rather than 50,000 points.

Airlines are not consistent with the amount of points needed for awards to similar destinations. For instance, one airline may require more points than other airlines for an award flight to Asia but less for an award flight to Hawaii. Another airline might offer First Class awards to Europe for much less than other airlines. For award flights to Brazil, one airline might "charge" 50,000 points, while another uses a partner airline and charges 85,000 points.

Once you are familiar with several programs, select a target destination and award. Your preferred airline should be convenient to use, fly to destinations that you intend to go, and have the best award structure. Book your award flight with that airline when you have enough points.

Here are requirements for First Class award flights to Asia:

Airline	One Ticket	Two Tickets
American	120,000	240,000
Delta	120,000	240,000
Northwest	80,000	160,000
United	120,000	180,000

A First Class award ticket to Asia requires 33 percent fewer points on Northwest. For two First Class tickets to Asia, United would be a better choice than Northwest, depending on convenience, quality, reliability, and point accumulation opportunities. For example, if your primary airport is O'Hare (Chicago), Dulles (Washington, DC), or San Francisco, then most of your flights will be on United rather than Northwest.

Consolidating flights on one airline enables you to accumulate points faster and get more rewards. Members that fly most are called very frequent flyers (VFF) or elite members. Not only do they accumulate points more quickly by flying more, but they also receive bonus points for being VFFs. For instance, a 100 to 150 percent bonus may be awarded to members flying over 100,000 miles in a year.

Frequent flyer points can be earned from several sources besides airline flights. Additional points can be earned by staying at hotels and using rental car companies that partner with the airline's frequent flyer program. You can also earn 10 points for every dollar spent at participating restaurants. Buying certain products, using the airline's credit card, or making telephone calls with the partner long distance service can earn more points.

For any offer, be aware of the requirements to earn points. Make sure that a product's price is not inflated more than the value of the bonus points. It is not a good deal to pay too much for a product simply to get more points. Frequent flyer points are worth 2 cents; 500 points are worth $10 and 1,000 points are worth $20. Product prices are often inflated for frequent flyer point offers. If 1,000 points are awarded with a $100 purchase, determine whether the product, like flowers, would cost less than $80 ($100 cost of flowers minus $20 value of points) elsewhere. Paying $100 for a $40 product in order to get $20 worth of frequent flyer points is not smart.

Figure 3.1
McCool Rule: Value of Frequent Flyer Points

Each frequent flyer point is typically worth 2 cents; 500 points are worth $10 and 1,000 points are worth $20. A 25,000 point award is worth $500.

Then again, paying an inflated price to get points could be a good strategy when only a few points are needed to reach an award level. Most of the time, it is less expensive than paying for an unnecessary flight. Some programs, including Continental's OnePass and United's Mileage Plus, allow members to buy points. OnePass members can buy up to 20% of the needed points in 1,000 point blocks for $25 each block. If you need 3,000 points for a 100,000 award, you can buy the points for $75.

To maximize the value of frequent flyer awards, redeem them for flights that would cost more than the award value. Basic awards for domestic flights are worth $500 (25,000 points at 2 cents per point). Using a domestic award for a flight that costs $199 is not a good value. Emergency, last minute, and business flights are usually expensive and ideal situations for redeeming frequent flyer awards.

Most airlines charge a fee for booking award flights with less than three weeks notice. Avoid paying the fee, and potential disappointment, by booking award flights more than three weeks before flying. Award flights can be booked up to 360 days in advance and free flights to popular destinations are booked very early. If needed, reserve award flights as far in advance as possible, then change the dates and times closer to the start of the trip. There is no fee for changing the dates and times of an award flight; completely changing the itinerary incurs only a $75 fee.

Discounted awards may be available for off-season flights or other promotions. A program may offer award flights to Europe for 40,000 points between January 15th and March 15th and 50,000 points for the rest of the year. Award flights may also be discounted when a new partner airline is introduced. Shorter award flights of 500 miles or less "cost" only 15,000 points on many airlines.

People flying once or twice a year should follow the principles in this book to get lower airfares, rather than trying to accumulate enough frequent flyer points for free flights. Frequent flyer programs are beneficial but it is not worth paying more for flights on a specific airline simply to earn frequent flyer points.

Figure 3.2
McCool Rule: Frequent Flyer Programs

1. Join Several Programs (they're FREE!)
2. Analyze Award Levels and Select a Preferred Program
3. Consolidate Points
4. Redeem Points for Emergency and Last-Minute Flights
5. Take Advantage of Non-Flight Point Accruals

Last-Minute Airfares

Many airlines offer discounted last-minute airfares. They are less expensive than full-fare prices but are rarely less than APEX fares.

Last-minute fares are useful for people who must travel without notice and can meet the restrictions. For instance, a last-minute fare of $109 between Washington, DC and Boston was much lower than the $390 full-fare but higher than the lowest price of $88. Passengers buying last-minute fares do not have to meet advance purchase requirements, but they do have to be extremely flexible. Most last-minute fares are advertised each week on Tuesday or Wednesday for flights on the upcoming Saturday and returning Monday or Tuesday. Travelers cannot use the last-minute fare to fly on Friday and return on Monday, or any other variation.

Most last-minute fares are for flights that are not full. The airlines want to increase the passenger load on relatively unpopular routes. Do not expect to find last-minute fares to popular destinations during peak travel periods. For example, during February, last-minute fares from Boston are usually for flights to New York, Philadelphia, and Washington, DC—not to Florida or the Caribbean.

Last-minute fare information can be found through various sources. They may be listed on a toll-free telephone number message, available by e-mail or fax, or advertised only on the Internet. Some airlines charge an additional $20 to book last-minute fares by telephone instead of using the Internet. **Appendix G** has instructions for requesting last-minute airfare information from various airlines and other sources.

Other strategies for last-minute flights can be found in the following sections:

Consolidators in Chapter 2

Frequent Flyer Programs in Chapter 3

Package Deals in Chapter 3

Tour Desks in Chapter 2

Co-Terminals

Using co-terminals[1] can result in lower airfares because airlines do not typically charge extra to use them. Instead, airlines determine the price of a co-terminal flight by averaging the fare to each airport. An example co-terminal flight is to Miami and back from Ft. Lauderdale. If the Miami flight costs $300 and the Ft. Lauderdale flight costs $320, the airline charges $310 for the co-terminal flight.

One advantage of using co-terminals is that you can select the best flights for each airport. In the above sample trip, assume that flights to Ft. Lauderdale are convenient but return flights are not. The opposite is true for Miami—great return flights but inconvenient flights there. The solution is a co-terminal flight, to Ft. Lauderdale and back from Miami.

The days, times, routings, or upgrade possibilities may be more convenient for one route than another. Perhaps flights to and from Miami are on Monday, Wednesday, and Friday, while flights to and from Ft. Lauderdale are on Tuesday, Thursday, and Saturday. Maybe all flights from Miami on the desired return date have connections while there is a non-stop flight from Ft. Lauderdale. Checking flights from each co-terminal allows you to get lower fares and select the most convenient flights.

A disadvantage of co-terminal flights is arranging transportation to the other airport. It may be a simple matter or a major hassle. For example, rates are higher for rental cars not returned to the pickup location. See also **Open Jaw Flights** in this chapter.

---

[1] Co-terminals - airports in the same city or metropolitan area. Examples include Miami & Ft. Lauderdale, San Francisco & Oakland, and Baltimore/Dulles/National.

Package Deals

A travel **package** combines several components—such as airfare, lodging, ground transportation, meals, and attractions—at a reduced price. The package price is lower than the total cost of its components. Many companies specialize in selling travel packages. Airlines also sell packages, usually from a Vacation Desk. See also **Tour Desks** in **Chapter 2**.

Packages are available to most popular tourist destinations, including Las Vegas, Orlando, Mexico, and the Caribbean. For instance, there are package deals from the United States to Australia and other South Pacific destinations each year. A flights costs $999 but a package—including the flight, seven nights lodging, and rental car—costs only $1,099.

Consider buying a travel package if it reduces the total cost of a trip. In the above example, the lowest airfare is $999. Lodging and transportation for a week would cost much more than $100, so the $1,099 package is an outstanding deal. However, not all package deals are a great value.

Travel packages have different restrictions than flights. Most packages do not require a Saturday night stay or have an advanced purchase requirement, for instance. They are an excellent source for last-minute trips, since the price may drop as the departure date approaches.

Always learn the details about every element of a travel package. Find out whether the flight is on a commercial or charter airline. Check on the hotel quality and rental car sizes. A supplier may offer several packages with various combinations—two or three meals a day; economy, midsize, or full size car; standard, deluxe, or luxury hotel.

Open Jaw Flights

Open jaw flights—flying into one city and back from another—offers travelers more flexibility than round-trip flights. Europe is ideal for open jaw flights because of its efficient and extensive train system. For instance, one can fly into Rome and return from London or into Amsterdam and back from Paris. An open jaw flight usually costs the average of each round-trip ticket; see the **Co-Terminals** example in this chapter.

Using a frequent flyer award for an open jaw flight is a great strategy. An open jaw award flight requires the same number of points as a round-trip flight. An award flight into Rome and back from London "costs" the same as a round-trip award flight to either London or Rome.

Costly rental car fees make open jaw trips too expensive for most U.S. routes. An exception is that most companies do not usually charge extra to return a car to another city in Florida. An open jaw flight into Tampa and from Miami (or any other pair of Florida cities) is possible.

A reasonable one-way fare between cities can make an open jaw flight possible. An open jaw flight from an East coast city to Portland (Oregon), and Las Vegas is possible because of low one-way fares between Las Vegas and Portland.

Open jaw flights can save travel time or let travelers see more during a trip. For an open jaw flight (from the East coast) into Los Angeles and back from Seattle, I used a frequent flyer award to travel from Monday to Friday—such a flight usually costs over $2,000. The rental car was $25 more per day than if it was returned to the pickup location. The additional cost of $125 (five days at $25 per day) can be justified, compared to the cost and time associated with driving back to Los Angeles from Seattle.

Also, more time can be spent visiting new areas instead of doubling back through already visited areas.

North American open jaw scenarios include flying into:

- Tampa and back from Orlando (or any pair of Florida cities)
- Minneapolis and back from Detroit
- Honolulu and back from Kona
- Vancouver and back from Toronto (train between cities)
- Seattle and back from Anchorage (cruise between cities)

Stopovers

Stopovers lower airfare costs by allowing passengers to visit more than one destination without buying separate tickets. Passengers visiting an intermediate city on a stopover trip get "two flights for the price of one." For example, instead of flying non-stop to Rome, a stop can be made in another European city, such as Amsterdam, London, or Paris.

Most airlines define a stopover as spending more than four hours between connecting flights. A **forced stopover** (or layover) occurs when the connecting flight is the following morning or later. This can occur for Caribbean flights with Miami being the stopover city, or for flights to Europe (see the Icelandair example below). The airline may include a free hotel stay for layover passengers. By taking the day's last flight to a stopover city, you might get free lodging.

An itinerary can be creatively altered to produce a stopover. Ask the agent about the valid cities and costs for stopovers on any route when researching fares. Requested stopovers usually cost $25 or $50. Honolulu is a valid stopover city between Los Angeles and Sydney, Australia. Instead of taking a non-stop Los Angeles-to-Sydney flight, book separate Los Angeles-to-Honolulu and Honolulu-to-Sydney flights for an extra $25.

Fares between the U.S. and Europe usually cost less on Icelandair than other carriers. Icelandair flights stop in Reykjavik, where the airline gives passengers a free night in a hotel. The stay in Iceland can be extended; passengers must pay the additional lodging costs and find an available seat on another flight to the final European destination.

Add-On Fares

Foreign airlines usually fly only from major gateway cities like New York and Los Angeles. Instead of buying a separate round-trip ticket to a gateway city to get a low transoceanic fare, save money with their add-on fare.

> **A major foreign airline offers flights to Cairo from New York for $500. They do not fly from any other U.S. city. They charge $550 to fly from Chicago and contract the Chicago-to-New York flights to another airline. Passengers pay less by using the add-on option instead of buying a separate Chicago-to-New York round-trip flight. Unfortunately, the $50 flight is not available by itself.**

Another type of add-on fare is for travelers buying cruises and packages. These add-on fares are usually good values because cruise and package suppliers negotiate volume discounts with the airlines. Add-on flights for cruises and packages are usually with certain carriers and for specific flights, which may be inconvenient; for example, a connecting flight instead of a non-stop flight. Always see if there is a less expensive or more desirable flight; you may want to redeem a frequent flyer award, use a certain carrier, or take advantage of a stopover to visit friends.

Companies offering add-on flights assume the risk of delay or cancellation. They must make arrangements to meet the ship, tour, or flight. However, passengers are responsible when independently arranged flights do not arrive in time to meet the ship, tour, or other flight. Consumers can minimize this risk with travel insurance (see **Chapter 5**).

Flights connecting to longer flights are a third type of add-on fare that can save you money (or provide luxurious service). For one trip, the best value between Sydney and Cairns, Australia was on a Qantas flight that continued to Tokyo. The Sydney-to-Cairns flight is usually not crowded as Qantas is simply repositioning the 747 aircraft for the long Cairns-to-Tokyo flight. There were only a handful of passengers and I ended up in Business Class; actually, I requested a seat close to the front and was accidentally, I think, given a Business Class seat assignment. U.S. examples include Varig flights between Washington, DC and Miami (continuing to Brazil) and United flights between San Francisco to Los Angeles (continuing to South America).

Air Passes and Coupon Books

When visiting larger countries or groups of countries, it is usually cheaper to buy an **air pass** instead of separate flights. Air pass holders are entitled to a certain number of flights during a specific time period—such as five flights in 30 days. Air passes are only available to non-residents and not sold in the country or region where they will be used. Passengers must buy air passes before arriving there.

Air passes are available for Brazil, India, the Caribbean, and other areas. There is even a "Visit USA" air pass.

Cathay Pacific has a $999 air pass for a 30-day period. It includes a round-trip flight from New York or Los Angeles to Hong Kong and flights to any of 17 Asian cities. It costs an additional $200 to fly in June or $300 to fly during the peak period or to extend the travel period an extra 60 days. Seniors and CyberTravelers—users that register on Cathay's Web site at < Cathay-usa.com >— receive a $100 discount.

An airline might sell air passes only in conjunction with a transoceanic flight. For example, a "See Europe" air pass is available only to passengers flying from New York to Paris. Other air passes, such as Caribbean or South Pacific island hoppers, are independent of other flights. In other words, passengers are not required to fly on a specific airline or route to buy and use the air pass.

Coupon books differ from air passes ONLY in who can use them. Air passes are for non-residents, while coupon books are available to everyone. Many coupon books are for particular market segments, such as seniors or students; most major U.S. airlines have coupon books for seniors and students. Airlines flying between the Hawaiian islands sell one type of coupon book only to Hawaiian residents and a different one to visitors. Most air passes and coupon books can be bought from travel agents, although some are only available through a specific airline, tourist bureau, or organization.

Coupon books usually contain four or eight coupons. Each coupon can be exchanged for a one-way flight, including any connections; a round-trip flight requires two coupons. Coupons from the "Visit USA" air pass—which costs $439 for three coupons, $489 for four, or $569 for five—can be redeemed for one-way flights within the continental United States. Flights to Alaska and Hawaii require two coupons or four coupons for the round-trip. Some airlines include cities in Canada, the Caribbean, and Mexico as part of the "continental U.S." Frequent flyer points are usually awarded for coupon flights, but not for air pass flights.

A further discount is possible with a book of eight coupons. Each coupon in the eight-coupon book costs less than each coupon in the four-coupon book. Make sure that you will use all eight coupons before buying the coupon book. Remember that you must complete travel within a year of buying the coupon book.

Coupons expire one year from the date they are issued, not the date of the first flight. In addition, reservations *must* be made two weeks in advance. The number of seats available to coupon users is limited, so reservations *should* be made as far in advance as possible. Coupons are issued with a specific name and cannot be shared. Identification is checked when buying air passes or coupon books, exchanging coupons for tickets, and checking in for flights.

Some airlines include tax in the price of coupon books, while others collect tax when passengers take the flights. In addition to comparing coupon book prices from various airlines, also check discount fares.

Always check if discounted fares are lower than coupon book prices. Coupon books are most effective for relatively expensive flights. An example:

> A senior couple is considering taking two trips from New York—to Los Angeles, Seattle, or both. With the airline's senior discount, a New York-to-Los Angeles flight costs $220 and a New York-to-Seattle flight costs $450. A senior coupon book costs $599 for four segments, essentially two round-trip flights for $300 each.

1. Two New York-to-Los Angeles flights cost $440, much less than the $599 coupon book. The couple can save $160 by buying the flights and NOT buying the coupon book.

2. Two New York-to-Seattle flights cost $900, much more than the $599 coupon book. The couple can save $300 by buying a coupon book instead of the flights with the senior discount.

3. One flight to each city will cost $670 ($220 + $450). The couple can save $70 by buying a coupon book.

One-Way Flights

It is almost always less expensive to buy round-trip rather than one-way tickets. In fact, almost all round-trip flights cost less than either of its one-way flights.

Following are specific situations when it *might* cost less to buy one-way tickets:

> Some routes have one-way fares for half the round-trip price. Discount airlines might offer one-way fares for many or all routes. Even one-way flights on SunTrips (see **Charter Flights** in Chapter 1) cost more than half of the round-trip price. There are not many routes where this scenario is true for major airlines.
>
> In May 2000, three discount airlines sold one-way New York-to-Los Angeles flights in all fare classes at half the round-trip price. Other airlines only sold one-way tickets for higher fare classes, such as 7-day APEX, full-fare, or Premium Class.

> From some foreign destinations, the return flight may cost less than the incoming flight, because of currency fluctuations, various taxes, or special agent/broker fares. You might be able to buy the return ticket in the U.S. and pick it up there.

Reasonable one-way fares allow travelers to have flexible travel plans, such as extended stays, no Saturday night stay requirement, or taking a train or driving in one direction. For most discounted fares, the trip must be completed within 30 days. To spend more than 30 days at a destination, two one-way flights (on such routes) might cost less than a round-trip ticket.

Standby Flights

Flying **standby** means not having a reservation for a flight—usually the next one—and requesting a seat on it. Passengers typically fly standby at a different time (earlier or later, different day) or on a different route (non-stop or direct). For instance, a business traveler buys a ticket two weeks in advance for a 7:00 P.M. flight, finishes work early on the return date, and requests a standby seat on the noon flight.

When seats are available, airlines usually allow standby passengers from other flights. When the flight has no available seats, standby requests are not honored. Ticketed passengers can continue requesting a standby seat on other flights. When the reserved flight is ready, then they can fly as scheduled. Unticketed passengers usually must pay full-fare and will receive seats before standby passengers.

Airline rules say that passengers with the lowest fares can request standby status for flights *only* on the same day of travel. Some discounted tickets allow no standby changes at all. If you have an emergency on a different day, request

U.S.ARMY®

a standby seat anyway. Most airlines are likely, but not guaranteed, to permit such standby requests; it depends on seat availability.

Air Hitch (800-834-9192, < AirHitch.org >) sells a different type of standby flight—for adventurous and flexible travelers. Air Hitch finds a flight to a region (Caribbean, Europe, or across North America) within a date range specified by the passenger. For example, someone wants to go to Europe on June 9th or 10th. Air Hitch might find a flight at noon on June 10th to Rome. A similar process occurs for the return flight and flights to the other areas. Fares from the East Coast to Europe are around $350 and to the Caribbean are about $200.

Round the World Tickets

If you intend to visit more than two international cities, a **Round the World (RTW)** ticket might save you money. RTW tickets are sold by most major airlines and by specialized travel agencies.

Basically, RTW flights are intended for continuous travel in one direction—east or west. Some airlines or companies charge extra for flights to Australia, South Pacific, Africa, Scandinavia, or South America. Others do not permit travel to these destinations on RTW itineraries. Some RTW itineraries might be limited to a maximum total distance, such as 25,000 miles or 42,000 kilometers. Additional distance is sometimes allowed for an extra fee.

RTW flights must be completed within one year from the first flight. The first segment must be reserved but subsequent flights do not have to be. However, changes after ticketing cost $25, so travelers should be certain of the itinerary before buying an RTW ticket.

Major U.S. airlines partner with international airlines for RTW flights. For instance, United Airlines' RTW flights are in conjunction with other Star Alliance partners—15 members as of June 2000—including Air New Zealand, All Nippon Airways, Lufthansa, SAS, and Singapore Airlines. For more information about the Star Alliance, visit < Star-Alliance.com > or < UAL.com >. You can fly on United across the Pacific and Atlantic Oceans and on other airlines within and between Asia and Europe. You could also exclusively use United, since they are one of only three airlines that can fly around the world without a partner; the others are Aeroflot and Air France.

RTW tickets sold by airlines are more expensive than those sold by specialized travel agencies. RTW agents develop itineraries by comparing flight options for each segment. The agents listed in **Appendix E** have been developing RTW trips for many years. Airline RTW ticket prices start at $2,500 for Economy Class, $3,500 for Business Class, and $5,000 for First Class. A basic itinerary through a specialized RTW agent costs about $1,000; flights are generally on major international airlines, such as China Airlines. Sample itineraries are listed in display advertisements of major newspaper Travel sections. The Web sites listed in **Appendix E** allow you to price various RTW itineraries.

Common strategies for RTW flights are to book:

1. Every flight in advance (for convenience and security)
2. Only the first flight (for complete flexibility)
3. Some flights (between these extremes)

Flexible travelers book only their first flight—maybe Los Angeles to Hong Kong—stay as long as they want in the initial city, and then pick the next destination based on flight availability, travel partner, or other preference.

When the trip begins, a RTW passenger may not even know which city to visit after the first. A tentative plan might be to stay in Hong Kong for a month and then fly to Bangkok. Instead, after a week in Hong Kong the traveler decides to go to Jakarta or Singapore. If the RTW itinerary already booked the Bangkok flight, then a flight to the other city must be found, the ticket reissued, and a change fee paid.

There may not even be a flight to the desired destination for several days or, in rare cases, weeks. This is a risk that flexible RTW travelers must accept. In the worst case, they will skip busy segments, such as Hong Kong to Singapore, and find an alternate destination, like New Delhi.

There are disadvantages for each strategy. The disadvantage of a flexible itinerary is that a desired flight may not be available or is at an inconvenient time. For example, there may be only one Hong Kong-to-Singapore flight per week. Disadvantages of booking all flights include paying $25 for each itinerary change.

Another strategy is to buy a basic RTW ticket and use Eurail or separate flights to visit other destinations. For example, a basic itinerary—New York to Hong Kong to London to New York—might cost $1,200. To add Bangkok, the RTW fare increases to $1,700. A Hong Kong-to-Bangkok round-trip flight might cost only $200, however. By buying the basic RTW ticket for $1,200 and the separate $200 ticket, you can save $300.

First and Business Class RTW flights are really good deals. A First Class flight between New York and Sydney costs approximately $8,000, while a First Class RTW flight stopping in Sydney (and many other cities) costs about $5,000. Compared to a First Class New York-to-Sydney flight, a First Class RTW ticket costs much less, permits travel to other international cities, and earns many more frequent flyer points.

Many RTW specialists charge an additional fee—usually three percent—for using a credit card. Consider using a credit card anyway, since it offers fraud protection and earns frequent flyer points. Ask about the frequent flyer issuance policy if it is an important consideration. Some airlines only issue frequent flyer points for flights leaving the United States. Other airlines may issue points only for certain routes.

Round the Pacific (or Circle the Pacific) flights are similar to RTW flights. Passengers fly clockwise or counterclockwise to their choice of cities along or in the Pacific Ocean, including Asia, Australia, North America, and South America. Popular destinations include Honolulu, Sydney, Hong Kong, Tokyo, and South Pacific islands.

Courier Flights

You can save over 50 percent on international airfares by flying as a **courier.** Free courier flights are possible but expect to pay a fraction of the lowest available fare. Common courier fares are $300 to $500 from California (Los Angeles or San Francisco) to Asia and $200 from New York to Europe. Courier fares are not much less than winter sale prices but can be much less than summer fares.

Courier companies ship time-sensitive materials and bulk goods to international destinations. They need people—called casual, international, or bonded couriers—on the flights in order to classify the cargo as passenger baggage. Customs clears passenger baggage first, followed by unaccompanied cargo (general freight). General freight can take more than three days to clear Customs and can be bumped from busy flights without advance notice. A cottage industry has developed, with courier companies selling cheap airline tickets and savvy travelers paying low fares to exotic destinations.

Most U.S. courier flights leave from New York, Los Angeles, and San Francisco. Occasional flights are available from Miami, Houston, Washington (DC), Boston, and other cities. **Appendix D** lists contact information for companies offering courier flights.

Courier flights can be reserved three months in advance, the day before the flight, or anytime in between. During spring and summer, flights are very popular and are often booked several weeks or months prior to the departure date. If you really want a courier flight to a specific international destination, book it three months in advance. If you simply want to travel, wait for a last-minute deal.

The price for an unbooked courier flight drops as the departure date approaches. The courier company has already paid for a passenger ticket and wants to recoup whatever money it can. The cargo cannot be shipped unless it is "accompanied" by a passenger. In rare cases, the company will let a courier fly for free; however, most have a policy to charge no less than $50 or $99. Flights under $100 are usually available only in the winter. You can negotiate a lower fare if you think the company is desperate.

Basic courier qualifications include following directions and being reliable, prompt, and presentable. Most courier companies have a dress code and no alcohol policy. Couriers must be over 21 (or 18), have a valid passport (and Visa for some countries), and submit a refundable deposit, usually $500, for the flight. The deposit is returned after the courier duties are completed.

Duties include meeting a company representative in each city, carrying a package of manifests (listings of package contents), and following instructions. Typical instructions include calling the office a couple of days before the return flight, meeting a representative in the airport, and wearing identification to be easily recognized.

Trade-offs include taking only carry-on baggage, checking in a couple of hours earlier than necessary, traveling alone, and dealing with possible last-minute changes. In the back of my mind, there was an insecure feeling that something could go wrong and I would get in trouble. Of course, nothing went wrong and it was a great experience.

Special benefits might include receiving frequent flyer points and having someone else check-in for you. This is especially welcome for the return flight; checking in at foreign airports can be nightmarish. After Chapter 6 is a story about my very successful courier trip.

Point Beyond Ticketing

For most destinations, particularly international, there is a lower airfare to a city beyond them. For example, airfares to Geneva, from New York and other U.S. cities, may cost more than airfares to Athens. Instead of buying a ticket to Geneva, save money by buying a round-trip flight to Athens with a stopover in Geneva. The intended destination (Geneva) becomes a stopover city instead of the final stop. See also **Stopovers** in this chapter.

Point beyond ticketing is the process of buying a ticket to that city beyond the intended destination in order to get a lower airfare. Spend just enough time—possibly just one day—in the "beyond" city to qualify for the lower price. Stop at your intended destination on the way to the beyond city, on the return flight, or both. Before buying a ticket, determine how long the airline allows you to stay in the stopover city and requires you to stay in the beyond city. Point beyond ticketing differs from hidden city ticketing because it is a legitimate offering by the airline.

4

Play to Win

Despite best efforts, you will not always get the lowest possible airfare when being flexible and resourceful. Sometimes you must be assertive—demand a lower airfare or stand up for your rights as a passenger—as a necessary part of the airfare game.

24-Hour Hold

You do not have to pay for a ticket when requesting a fare quote or when making a reservation. A reservation can be held for at least 24 hours, during which time you should shop for lower airfares. Most agents will say something like, "This fare is not guaranteed until purchased and your reservation will expire tomorrow at midnight."

Some agents try to close the sale without mentioning the grace period ("which credit card will you use?"). In these situations, simply request that your reservation be held. Say something like, "Please hold this reservation and I will call later to buy the ticket."

A 24-hour hold is actually more than 24 hours because the reservation usually expires at midnight on the following day. For example, a reservation made at 4:00 P.M. is valid until midnight the next day, 32 hours later. See the next section of this chapter, **A 24-Hour Extension,** to learn about holding a reservation an extra day.

During the **24-hour hold,** check for lower airfares or better flights. Call other airlines, consolidators, and discount agents, use the Internet, and ask if any can offer a lower fare. Check the Internet for prices, number of available seats, and on-time performance of flights. If there is no lower fare or better flight, then complete the on-hold reservation by buying the ticket.

Use the 24-hour hold period to arrange other parts of your trip, check with your travel partner, or even make sure that you want to take the flight. Synchronize other arrangements—such as hotel and rental car—with the reserved flights.

When possible, select flights that maximize the value of hotels and rental cars. Since most hotels do not let guests check in before 3:00 P.M., a flight arriving around 4:00 P.M. allows you to immediately check into your room. A flight with a morning arrival puts you at the destination too early to check into the hotel.

Also, select flights that will enable you to take advantage of lower rental car rates. Rental car companies charge for whole days, so return a car as close as possible to the time it was picked up. For example, if you pick up the car at

5:00 P.M. and return it at 8:00 A.M. another day, you pay for eight hours (8:00 A.M. to 5:00 P.M.) that the car is not being used. A return flight closer to 5:00 P.M. allows more travel time without incurring any extra rental car fees.

By adjusting flight times and car pickup and drop-off times, you might qualify for a weekly rate. A weekly rate—for a rental period between five and seven days—is almost always a bargain compared to daily rates. For example, paying the daily rate of $55 for five days (total of $275) costs almost twice the weekly rental rate of $139.

A daily rate is charged for anything less than one day. Keeping a car for four days and three hours results in the daily rate being charged for five days. Using the above rates, keeping the car for an extra day can save you almost $140 ($275 - $139).

Make a reservation, even if the lowest possible airfare is not available. Periodically check during the 24-hour hold period to see if a lower fare becomes available. Many people will make a reservation but not buy the ticket for some reason—cannot take time from work, dates are inconvenient, or car or hotel costs too much. However, the seat remains reserved until the passenger or travel agent cancels the itinerary, or, most likely, the unticketed reservations are cleared. Knowing when the airline's computer system clears reservations gives you a better chance to get a good fare, especially during periods of heavy demand.

Airlines usually clear unticketed reservations—those past the 24-hour hold—from the computer reservation system (CRS) each day around midnight. When making a reservation, ask the agent to clarify exactly when the hold expires—"midnight my time" or PST, EST, or when. Based on your location, reservations expire and unticketed seats become available anytime between 9:00 P.M. and 3:00 A.M.; later or earlier outside the continental United States.

To increase the likelihood of getting a low fare, call the airline just after the time that unticketed reservations are cleared, especially during fare wars and other high-demand periods. Let your location work in your favor—people on the West coast can call before going to sleep while East coasters would have to stay up late or wake early. Even calling in the morning gives you a better chance to get a scarce low airfare over someone calling later in the day.

One disadvantage of a 24-hour hold is the possibility that the fare will increase before the ticket is bought. Airlines can (and do) change the fare structure whenever they want. However, most fare changes happen just after midnight. Always remember that no fare is guaranteed until the ticket is purchased.

A 24-hour hold will not work if the time extends into another APEX (advanced purchase) period. For example, if the lowest fare requires tickets to be purchased 14 days in advance, then the hold cannot extend to 13 days before the flight. In other words, reservations made 14 days prior to a flight (for 14-day APEX fares) must be purchased the same day and cannot be held for the 24-hour hold period.

An exception to the 24-hour hold period is a **Special Instant Purchase Fare**. Airlines created this fare class to encourage consumers to buy the ticket when getting an airfare quote. These fares are available only from the airlines; travel agents, unfortunately, cannot book them. An example is a $276 instant purchase fare for New York-to-Los Angeles flights on two airlines, while the next lowest fare is $404.

A 24-Hour Extension

If the 24-hour hold (see previous section) is about to expire and you are not ready to buy a ticket, then request that the reservation be held for an additional day. The extension should be given unless there is a fare war and there is high demand for your reserved, but unticketed, seat.

When the airline will not allow another hold, make another reservation. You create an extension because the new reservation expires a day later. This tactic only works if the new reservation still meets all of the APEX requirements and seats are available at the same low airfare.

By the way, you can request the extension anytime during the day; you do not have to wait until midnight. Here are a couple of sample conversations for requesting a 24-hour extension.

Agent: Thank you for calling XYZ Airlines.
You: My reservation is expiring tonight but I am not ready to buy. Can you extend it until tomorrow?
Agent: What is the flight or reservation number?
You: Flight 123 on March 4th.
Agent: Your last name?
You: Flyer.
Agent: OK, I found your reservation. Flight 123 on March 4th, leaves Newark at 9:10 A.M. and arrives Los Angeles at 12:15 P.M. Flight 987 on March 10th, leaves LAX at 8:20 A.M. and arrives Newark at 5:45 P.M. The fare is $250 and must be ticketed by midnight tonight.
You: Yes that's it. Can you extend the reservation until tomorrow? Thank you.

Section One: Agent says, "YES"

Agent: The ticket must be bought by midnight tomorrow.
-or-
Agent: I can give you until noon tomorrow.

You: Great. Thank you.
Agent: No airfare is guaranteed until ticketed. If you do not purchase your ticket by midnight (or noon) tomorrow, the reservation will expire.
You: OK. Thank you.
Agent: Thank you for calling XYZ Airlines. Good-bye.

Section Two: Agent says, "NO"

Agent: I'm sorry, this reservation must be ticketed by midnight tonight.
You: There is no way that I can extend my reservation?
Agent: I'm afraid not. If you do not ticket this reservation by midnight it will automatically cancel.

Your Choice...

You: OK, thank you for checking.
-or-
You: In that case, I will buy the ticket.
-or-
You: Thank you. I will call back before midnight.

This is an opportunity to make another reservation. If you make a new reservation, call back and cancel the first one. If you cannot extend the old reservation or make a new one, then you must decide whether to buy the ticket or let the reservation expire.

Ask

ASK, ASK, ASK for the lowest possible price. Always specifically ask for the "lowest possible airfare"—use the words "lowest possible airfare." If you ask for economy, APEX, or discounted fares, you may not get the lowest airfare. Tell the agent that your travel plans are flexible and you want the lowest possible airfare. Provide a range of dates if possible.

For example, instead of saying:

> "I would like a Coach Class seat for flight 1234 on November 11th."

say:

> "I would like the lowest possible airfare between Charlotte and Las Vegas for mid-November. Ideally, I would like to depart on November 11th and return on November 17th but my plans are flexible. I really want the lowest airfare. Thank you."

After the agent provides a fare quote, ask if it is the lowest available fare for that time period. When a fare quote is higher than expected, ask how to get a lower airfare. For example, fares are usually less when changing airlines, airports, dates, times, or other factors (see **Chapter 1**).

Back-to-Back Tickets

> **WARNING**: Back-to-back tickets are against most airline's rules. In the rare instances of passengers being caught using this type of ticket, airlines charge them or the travel agents the difference between the paid fare and the full-fare. The airline can also terminate the frequent flyer account, eliminate all

earned points and awards, prohibit violators from flying on the airline, and pursue criminal action.

When you cannot stay at your destination for a weekend—and thus cannot qualify for most discounted airfares—you might save money by buying two round-trip tickets. The first ticket gets you to the destination and the second ticket returns you. The trick is to only use the first flight from each round-trip ticket and not take the return flights. You simply do not take the second flights or, perhaps, you try to use them for another trip.

To make **back-to-back tickets** work, it is critical to correctly arrange the return flights. The return flights must conform to fare rules—including length of stay, advanced purchase, and specific dates and times. Return flights can be a week later or whenever, as long as the round-trip fare is the lowest possible. It is possible to arrange the return flights for another trip but the main purpose is to pay less for your current trip.

The second round-trip is the reverse of the first one; starting from the destination on the day you want to return home. As with the first flight, arrange this return flight to get the lowest possible airfare, even though it will not be taken.

Back-to-back ticketing might best be explained with an actual example:

You need to fly from Atlanta to Seattle on a Monday and return on Friday, four days later. The lowest possible airfare for this itinerary with no Saturday night stay is $1,300. With a Saturday night stay, the fare plummets to $275. Buying two separate round-trips (for $550) costs $750 less than the $1,300 flight.

The first round-trip flight leaves Atlanta on Monday and returns (from Seattle) a week later*. The second round-trip flight departs Seattle on Friday (four days after the Monday flight) and returns (from Atlanta) a week later*. From each itinerary, use the first flight and do not use the return flight. The two round-trip flights should be on different airlines to minimize the possibility of being detected and subsequently charged the full-fare rate—$1,300 for each flight or $2,600 total.

* Arrange the return flights to get the lowest possible fare. The return flight usually must be within 30 days of the initial flight. If you do not intend to use the return flights, set them up for the following week.

If you have a second trip planned, arrange the return flights to coincide with those travel dates. To make the same trip to Seattle two weeks later, for instance, set up back-to-back flights as follows:

First Round-trip Ticket:

Atlanta-to-Seattle: Monday (flight #1)

Seattle-to-Atlanta: Friday + 2 weeks (flight #4)

Second Round-trip Ticket:

Seattle-to-Atlanta: Friday (flight #2)

Atlanta-to-Seattle: Monday + 2 weeks (flight #3)

The second round-trip is nested inside the first one. That is, both flights from the second round-trip are taken between the flights of the first round-trip. Back-to-back tickets are also called nested tickets.

The airlines have taken severe measures against travel agents issuing, and passengers buying, back-to-back tickets. On the other hand, travel agencies are upset because airlines encourage some customers to buy back-to-back tickets but penalize travel agents that sell the tickets.

To minimize the risks of back-to-back tickets, book flights on different airlines and with different travel agents. Risks of using back-to-back tickets include:

- Additional fee (up to full-fare) may be charged
- Frequent flyer account can be terminated
- Other penalties can be imposed

Figure 4.1
McCool Jewel: Back-to-Back Tickets on Southwest

While most airlines penalize travelers using back-to-back tickets, Southwest Airlines specifically states on its Web site:

"Hidden city" and "back to back" reservations and tickets are authorized for travel on Southwest Airlines.

Backup Plan

Particularly during peak travel periods, it can be useful to make a second reservation, in case something goes wrong with the first one. The backup reservation should be on a different airline. Peak travel periods include fare wars and around Thanksgiving, Christmas, and other holidays.

Cancel pending reservations after buying a ticket. Typically, unticketed itineraries automatically cancel at midnight (see **24-Hour Hold** in this chapter). It is good practice to allow other passengers every opportunity to get lower airfares.

> **One September I was fortunate to get the "last cheap seat" for a popular flight near Christmas. I also made a second reservation with another airline—just in case something went wrong with the first one. I confirmed the first reservation and went to my travel agent to get the ticket issued.**
>
> **She called the airline and was told there was no record of my reservation. I was more than annoyed! I figured there was a waiting list to buy the cheap seats and the airline did not want to forfeit commission to my travel agent. The airline would make more money if they, rather than my travel agent, booked the ticket. Whether true or not, that was my thought at the time.**
>
> **After many flights with this airline, I had earned a very frequent flyer status. When the airline's agent could not find my reservation, I had the travel agent tell him I will fly on another airline and that, as an elite member, I expected better service. He suddenly found the reservation and my travel agent issued the ticket.**
>
> **My travel agent was surprised that I made two reservations for the same trip AND was willing to pass up a good travel deal. Everything worked out with my initial reservation, but I was prepared in case it did not.**

Bumping

Airlines regularly sell more tickets than the number of available seats. Imagine that happening in another industry! Historical data models show that some ticketed passengers will not show up for a flight; the actual number varies for each flight. Occasionally, not enough reservations are canceled, there are too many passengers, or the flight switches to a smaller aircraft. Whatever the reason, when there are more passengers than seats, the flight is **overbooked**.

When a flight is overbooked, the airline first asks for volunteers to take a different flight. The airline rebooks **bumped** passengers on the next possible flight—to the passenger's final destination—and compensates them with a combination of travel certificates, upgrades, cash, free meals, or hotel rooms. The amount paid to volunteers—called **voluntary denied boarding** compensation—depends on many factors, including additional time needed to get to the final destination, demand for seats, airline policy, and volunteer's negotiation. Compensation also varies between domestic and international flights.

In rare instances when there are not enough volunteers, the airline chooses which passengers will be bumped. **Involuntary denied boarding passengers** usually include those not checked in (late arrivals) or not in their seat (late boarders). Passengers that do not confirm international flights according to the airline's policy—usually 48 or 72 hours prior—are also potential targets. Involuntarily bumped passengers receive involuntary denied boarding compensation, which is less negotiable than the voluntary type.

Most overbooked flights occur during holiday and peak periods or on introductory and fare war routes.

Bump-able situations include:

1. Holiday flights. The busiest travel days are usually the day before and the Sunday after Thanksgiving. Flights around other holidays can also be overbooked. Many flights for various routes are overbooked on these days.

2. Peak leisure routes. Los Angeles-to-Las Vegas flights on Friday nights and flights to Florida during Spring Break are very popular and can be overbooked.

3. Peak business routes. San Francisco-to-Los Angeles, New York-to-Chicago, and other popular business routes can be overbooked on Friday afternoons—when travelers are returning home—and other times.

4. Introductory routes. Airlines overbook flights when entering a new market and establishing new routes. They offer low fares to entice consumers but sell too many tickets. I was bumped twice from one airline's introductory flights between California and Japan. One time I was bumped from a Tokyo-to-Los Angeles flight. Another time the Los Angeles-to-Hawaii segment of a flight that continued to Tokyo was overbooked. For details, see the story following Chapter 6.

To avoid being bumped, confirm travel plans, check in early, remain in the boarding gate area to hear any announcements, and board as soon as possible to claim your seat; in most double-booked seating assignments the first occupant keeps the seat. If you are involuntarily bumped, negotiate the best possible compensation package.

Figure 4.2
McCool Rule: How to Avoid Being Bumped

1. Confirm and Reconfirm Itineraries
2. Check In Early
3. Stay in Boarding Area to Hear Announcements
4. Board as Early as Possible

To increase your chance of being bumped, volunteer early, check in periodically with the gate agent, look professional, and be pleasant. When checking in, ask if the flight will be full. If the agent says the flight is expected to be full, ask if it will be overbooked. Request to be listed as a volunteer at that point. Say "my travel plans are flexible" rather than "I want to be bumped."

Volunteer to be bumped for all flight segments when checking in for your first one. A connecting flight may be overbooked and you will already be listed as a bump volunteer before getting to the connecting airport. After being listed, stay in the boarding area and pay attention to all announcements. Occasionally ask the gate agent if volunteers are still needed or if you should board the plane.

Some people predict overbooked flights and fly specifically to be bumped. In other words, they buy tickets on busy flights expecting to be bumped and receive compensation.

Figure 4.3
McCool Rule: How to Get Bumped

1. Volunteer Early
2. Be Professional and Pleasant
3. Confirm Status
4. Buy Seats on Overbooked Flights

When bumped from a flight, request a travel voucher instead of a free travel certificate. Flights discounted with a voucher earn frequent flyer points while free flights do not. Before accepting a compensation package when being bumped, make sure you are assigned a confirmed seat on the next flight. If the airline cannot guarantee a convenient alternate flight, request a seat on another airline's flight. If an alternate flight has no Coach Class seats, ask for a First Class seat.

Bumped passengers are entitled to compensation other than what is offered. Request meal or hotel vouchers, passes to the airline's club lounge, or free telephone calls. If the flight is very overbooked and there are not enough volunteers, try to negotiate additional or better compensation—including cash, frequent flyer points, or travel vouchers. For instance, the compensation for an overbooked holiday flight should be more than for a Friday evening leisure route.

Emergency Flights

Passengers booking flights at the last moment (within a couple days of departure) pay the highest fares. However, airlines offer discounted fares to people that must fly with no prior notice because of the death or serious illness of a family member. Rules for emergency flights vary but expect to pay 50 to 75 percent of the full-fare price. Some airlines waive the advanced purchase restriction and offer the lowest possible airfare in case of emergency. See also **Compassion Fares** in Chapter 2.

Using frequent flyer awards for emergency flights is an excellent strategy. Two methods of using frequent flyer awards for emergency flights are:

1. Redeem frequent flyer points. Frequent flyer programs charge $25 to $100 to book an award flight within 21 days of departure. Most programs do not charge any fee to book an award flight more than 21 days away.

2. Modify an existing award flight. You can book an award flight about a year in advance—360 days for most programs. If an emergency occurs before the award flight, you can completely change the itinerary, including the route, for a $50 fee. There is no charge to change only the dates of travel of an award ticket, as long as the route stays the same.

Here is a comparison of typical costs:

1. A last-minute cross-country flight typically costs $1,500
2. Bereavement fare costs $750 to $1,200
3. Consolidator fare costs $300 to $700
4. NEW award flight costs $100 (expedite booking fee)
5. CHANGED award flight costs $50 (change fee, if the new routing is different) or $0 (same route)

The best deal is to use frequent flyer points. However, not everyone has frequent flyer points. Many consolidators sell discounted airfares with no restrictions, particularly useful for emergency scenarios. See **Consolidators** in Chapter 2.

Hidden City Tickets

> **WARNING**: Hidden city tickets are against most airline's rules. In the rare instances of passengers being caught using this type of ticket, airlines charge them or the travel agents the difference between the paid fare and the full-fare. The airline can also terminate the frequent flyer account, eliminate all earned points and awards, prohibit violators from flying on the airline, and pursue criminal action.

Especially for business travelers, it is annoying and absurd that fares for connecting flights cost less than one of the segments. For example, Boston-to-Chicago flights are cheaper than Boston-to-Milwaukee flights that connect in Chicago. In other words, it costs less to fly Boston-to-Chicago-to-Milwaukee than Boston-to-Chicago. So, some business travelers will book the connecting flight (Boston to Milwaukee), use only the part they need (Boston to

Chicago), skip the second flight (Chicago to Milwaukee), and discard the unused ticket.

Hidden city tickets can work only for a passenger on a one-way flight with carry-on luggage. Checked baggage is marked to go to the final destination; passengers cannot check bags and skip a connecting flight. When someone misses any flight segment, the airline cancels the rest of the itinerary; a hidden city ticket only works for one-way flights. The best candidates for hidden city tickets are hub airports—like Chicago, as in the above example—where most flights originate or connect.

Leisure travelers should not need to use hidden city tickets because discounted fares have lower prices. Point beyond ticketing is a strategy that leisure travelers might use. It is similar to hidden city ticketing, except that the second flight is actually taken. See **Point Beyond Ticketing** in Chapter 3.

Figure 4.4
McCool Jewel: Hidden City Tickets on Southwest

While most airlines penalize travelers using hidden city tickets, Southwest Airlines specifically states on its Web site:

"Hidden city" and "back to back" reservations and tickets are authorized for travel on Southwest Airlines.

A hidden city example (all flights are on TWA):

$981, Los Angeles-to-St. Louis, one-way

$291, Los Angeles-to-St. Louis-to-Kansas City, one-way

$455, Los Angeles-to-St. Louis, round-trip

This round-trip fare must be booked 14 days before the flight, which business travelers cannot do.

A business traveler saves $690 by buying the hidden city ($291 flight) ticket, flying from Los Angeles to St. Louis, and NOT flying from St. Louis to Kansas City. The traveler will have to find a similar hidden city route for the return trip.

Inconvenience Compensation

Passengers can request compensation from the airline for discomfort or inconvenience—flight delay, poor service, and other reasons. An airline employee will sometimes issue a voucher to a disgruntled passenger. This section explains these vouchers. Other times, passengers must go through a process to request compensation for a problem. The process is covered in **When Things Go Wrong** in Chapter 5.

An **inconvenience voucher** is a certificate given to disgruntled passengers by at least one major U.S. airline. The vouchers can be applied to future flights, similar to Dollar Off coupons (see **Discount Certificates** in Chapter 2). Passengers that experience problems can request a voucher from any employee, particularly customer service agents.

Most inconvenience vouchers are issued for delayed flights. Vouchers could also be requested for poor service, unexplained flight delays, fare decrease ineligible for a refund, or errors or disagreements (incorrect or lost reservation, lost upgrade confirmation). Airlines usually balk at giving vouchers for something out of its control, such as weather delays. On the other hand, airlines want to improve customer satisfaction and might see this as an opportunity to do so.

Airline staff sometimes voluntarily issues vouchers. Without asking, I received a certificate when a free (award) flight was delayed. Another time, I was given a voucher after volunteering to be bumped and the flight was not overbooked—a "Thank you" gesture from the airline.

Only one voucher can be applied to a round-trip fare. Travel agents and airline reservation agents can process them. Vouchers are valid for one year and are not transferable; however, airline staff rarely enters the name or date when issuing a voucher. When I had too many vouchers, I would give some to friends and even my travel agent.

When using an inconvenience voucher, the discount is applied before the tax, making the savings greater than face value. For example, when applying a $25 voucher to a $98 flight, the final cost is about $71.50 instead of $73.

Matching Fares

This is a corollary to asking for the lowest possible airfare (see **Ask** in this chapter). You may get a lower fare by asking an airline to match another airline's price. The air travel industry is very competitive and each airline wants you to fly with them.

An example is unadvertised Special Instant Purchase fares offered by some airlines. Between New York and Los Angeles, two airlines offer a $275 fare to passengers buying a ticket during the same session as receiving a fare quote. The lowest fare on other airlines is over $400. With this information, call your favorite airline and ask if they will match the $275 fare.

Figure 4.5
McCool Jewel: Matching Fares

Ask your favorite airline to match a fare offered by another carrier. Indicate that you are a loyal customer (if you are) and prefer to fly with them. In many cases, they will match the competitor's fare.

Rebooking Flights

Passengers must pay $50 or $75 to make changes to discounted airfares (that is, anything except full-fare). The new flight must still meet the fare requirements or you will be charged the current fare (usually higher) in addition to the service fee.

When a fare decreases, most airlines allow passengers to rebook existing tickets at the lower fare. The airline issues a travel voucher for the fare difference; these travel vouchers expire two years after the date of issue. Travel agents can sometimes get a refund for the fare difference—instead of a travel voucher—but only for tickets that they issued. Passengers must meet the restrictions of the new lower fare as well as find available seats. Tickets bought from the airline must be reissued at an airport or ticket office rather than by telephone.

Some discounted tickets can be rebooked without paying a change fee. One airline may have a no-fee change policy for all flights, while another might not charge for ticket changes for flights on certain competitive routes. Ask the airline about their policy for making changes to tickets, particularly if you are uncertain of your travel dates. You may decide to buy a slightly more expensive fare if the airline does not charge for itinerary changes.

Unrestricted tickets, including Premium Class and full-fare, never have reissue fees. If one does, avoid the rebooking fee by simply buying a ticket for the desired flight and getting a refund for the old ticket.

> **You bought four $300 tickets a month ago but recently discovered a $210 fare for the same route. The departure date is two months away, so call the airline and ask if the new lower fare applies to your tickets. An agent says that seats are available at the new low fare, but you must go to the airport or city ticket office to rebook the tickets. The airline reissues your tickets at the lower price and gives you four $90 vouchers that can be applied to future flights. They must be used within two years.**

Split Ticketing

Split ticketing or split-city ticketing is buying two separate round-trip tickets for a single trip. The two round-trip flights take advantage of the airline's pricing schemes to create a lower total airfare. In addition to paying less, there may be other benefits to booking split-city tickets.

An example to illustrate the split ticketing strategy:

A friend received quotes of $600 to fly from San Jose, California to Cabo San Lucas, Mexico. I checked a couple of sources and confirmed that $600 was the lowest available fare. I also discovered that all flights connected through Los Angeles or Phoenix. I then researched two separate itineraries:

1. (San Jose-to-Los Angeles) AND (Los Angeles-to-Cabo)

- OR -

2. (San Jose-to-Phoenix) AND (Phoenix-to-Cabo)

At the time, Los Angeles-to-Cabo flights cost $198 and San Jose-to-Los Angeles flights cost $98. Los Angeles also offered more options—airlines and flights—so I concentrated on using it as the interim airport. Splitting the trip into two round-trips would cost $296 ($198 + $98). By buying two tickets, anyone could save 50%—over $300 ($600 - $296).

These split ticket flights were not less convenient, since the $600 fare required changing planes in Los Angeles (or Phoenix) anyway. In fact, there were a couple of advantages to buying split tickets for this trip.

One advantage was that my friend was able to book flights with preferred airlines and add points to active frequent flyer accounts. Only two airlines offered San Jose-to-Cabo flights and both were undesirable from a frequent flyer standpoint. Several airlines offered San Jose-to-Los Angeles and Los Angeles-to-Cabo flights, giving her more choices.

Another advantage of a split ticket itinerary is that you can create stopovers, which are not permitted on most discounted round-trip flights. For instance, fly from San Jose to Los Angeles the night before flying to Cabo. Spend a day in Los Angeles before taking an afternoon Los Angeles-to-Cabo flight. The time spent in Los Angeles is a created stopover. Create a similar stopover with the return flights. Stopovers counter the major problem with split ticketing, possibly missing the connection if either flight into Los Angeles is canceled or delayed.

With split tickets you usually must claim your baggage from the first airline, carry it to the second airline, and check in with the second one. If the airlines have an interline agreement, your baggage will automatically be transferred. Bringing only carry-on baggage is the best way to eliminate this disadvantage, but you still must check in with the second airline.

My split ticket trips have included San Francisco-to-Kona, Hawaii (through Honolulu), and Monterey-to-Miami (through Los Angeles) flights. The Honolulu-to-Kona flights were actually interisland flights. Major airlines fly directly to Kona at a much higher fare (usually) than to Honolulu. Monterey-to-Miami flights are available on a couple of airlines, but I had a promotional First Class seat on a Los Angeles-to-Miami flight with an airline that did not fly from Monterey. Another time, I got a very low airfare between Los Angeles and Miami with that same airline. It was worth buying separate Monterey-to-Los Angeles flights in order to get great deals on another airline.

Standby

Instead of paying the $50 or $75 fee to rebook a ticket (see **Rebooking Flights** in this chapter), you can usually **standby** for a flight on the same day at no cost. Ask the airline if standby travel is allowed for your ticket. Most, but not all, airfares permit same-day standby changes.

After verifying that your fare is eligible for standby travel, ask if there are available seats on an earlier or later flight, whichever you want. Unless you have a full-fare ticket, an agent will not be able to confirm a standby seat over the telephone. However, the agent can advise you whether to attempt to fly standby. The agent should tell you if there is no chance of getting a standby seat, so that you do not waste time going early to the airport.

After confirming the likelihood of flying standby on a specific flight, go to the airport at least an hour before its departure. You may have to wait to see how full the flight is, but often the check-in or gate agent will be able to confirm a seat assignment for you.

Even if your fare does not allow standby changes, an agent may override the restriction and let you fly. It depends on the flight load, agent demeanor, and your attitude. If one agent says no, asking another might work in your favor.

Example 1:

> You have a 7:00 P.M. flight but will be ready to leave at noon. Call the airline and ask if earlier flights are likely to have standby seats. The agent says that the 2:00 and 4:00 P.M. flights look good for standby passengers. Go to the airport at 1:00 PM, check in, and get a seat on the 2:00 P.M. flight, because the plane is nearly empty.

Example 2:

> Your fare is "non-refundable and non-changeable" but you want to return home three days early. Go to the airport and ask to fly standby on the next flight. You can try an emotional plea—such as an emergency at home or work—but the decision is usually based on the availability of seats. If the flight has available seats, the agent is likely to let you fly. You will not get a seat on a crowded flight. I once flew standby a couple of days early with a non-changeable ticket. However, the return route had two connections and took an extra few hours.

5

Stay Ahead

After getting the lowest possible airfare, try to do everything you can to keep it. This chapter discusses how to avoid travel scams and rip-offs, keep low airfares and enjoy the flights, and effectively handle problem situations.

Confirming and Reconfirming Flights

Confirming your itinerary is the most effective way to eliminate potential problems. By confirming your reservation, you can fix duplicate, incorrect, or missing seat assignments, lost reservations, and other problems before they occur. You also can verify that your itinerary includes your frequent flyer number and special meal request. If the current fare is lower than when you bought your ticket, you can request a refund or travel voucher. It is easier to fix problems by telephone before the flight than when checking in at the airport—especially if the gate agents are solving other passenger's problems.

Most airlines require that passengers confirm domestic flights 24 hours in advance and international flights 48 or 72 hours before departure. Reservations can be confirmed by calling the airline. **Appendix A** lists telephone numbers for making reservations and checking automated flight information for the ten largest U.S. airlines; itineraries can be confirmed through either number. Passengers not confirming flights, especially return flights to the U.S., risk losing seat assignments. Unconfirmed passengers can be completely bumped from an overbooked flight (see **Bumping** in Chapter 4).

Confirm flights closer to departure time in addition to as recommended by the airline. For instance, confirm an afternoon flight a couple of hours before departure. If the flight is canceled or delayed, then it is better to reschedule it over the phone than at the airport (see also **When Things Go Wrong** in this chapter).

In addition to confirming dates, times, and seat assignments prior to the flight, passengers can request class upgrades, itinerary changes, special meals, or standby status. For example, ask whether it is feasible to standby for an earlier flight. You are more likely to be successful requesting some changes by telephone instead of at the airport.

Figure 5.1
McCool Rule: What to Confirm BEFORE Buying a Ticket

Cost
Passenger's Name (must match spelling on ID card)
Flight Times (e.g., 9:00 A.M. versus 9:00 P.M.)
Dates of Travel (6/7 or 7/6, Tu. or Th.)
Connections or Stops (non-stop or direct)
Time Between Connections[1]
Airports (Dallas or Dulles, IAD or DCA, MSY or MSP)[2]
Flight Numbers
Airline (AA or UA, UA or US, CO or CX, QA or NZ[3])[4]
Frequent Flyer Account Number
Special Meal
Seat Assignment

It is better to discover and correct errors—especially the wrong day or airport—before paying for your ticket.

---

[1] Some airports, like Dallas (DFW), require a minimum time between connecting flights, like 25 minutes.
[2] These codes are for Washington Dulles (IAD), Ronald Reagan Washington National (DCA), New Orleans (MSY), and Minneapolis/St. Paul (MSP).
[3] Codeshare – many airlines sublet seats from other airlines. For example, Air New Zealand might sell seats to passengers, but the flight is on a Qantas airplane.
[4] These airline codes are American (AA), United (UA), US Airways (US), Continental (CO), Continental Express (CX), Qantas (QA), and Air New Zealand (NZ). Many airline codes are listed **Appendix A** and **Appendix B**.

Figure 5.2
McCool Rule: What to Confirm AFTER Buying a Ticket

Cost (ask for a refund if the current fare is lower)
Seat Assignment (request a different one if desired)
Flight Times (note any changes)
Dates of Travel
Time Between Connections
Flight Numbers (note any changes)
Frequent Flyer Account Number
Special Meal
Gate Location(s)
First Class Upgrade
Waitlist Status
Flight Status (on the day of travel)

Double-check all flight information and note any changes. Improve your situation (seat assignment or class upgrade) if you can. Checking the flight status on the day of travel helps if it is delayed or canceled.

Flight Comfort Tips

The pressured, recirculated air sucks moisture from your body, causing fatigue, headaches, and other ailments. Alcohol and soft drinks also cause the body to crave more water. Try to drink a pint of water for every hour on an airplane. Bring your own water bottle and refill it during the flight. Request bottled water when the flight attendants come by with the drink cart.

Frequently stretch your legs. Request an aisle seat so that you can get up without bothering other passengers in your row. Walk around the airplane or just stand in the aisle. Legs get cramped on long flights so move around as much as possible.

Effectively pack your carry-on bags. Bring enough water and snacks for long flights. Pack entertainment, including books, music, crossword puzzles, or playing cards. Place essentials, such as medications, in carry-on bags in case your checked baggage is lost. Many people pack the next day's clothing and supplies in their carry-on baggage.

Passengers can switch seats once the airplane door closes. If the airplane is not full and you do not like your seat, then move to a desirable one when the door is shut. You can anticipate which seats will remain empty and move to one before the door closes. However, if the assigned passenger shows, then you must find another seat or retreat to your original one.

Figure 5.3
McCool Rule: Tips for Comfortable Flights

1. Drink plenty of water.
2. Frequently stretch your legs.
3. Pack entertainment and essentials in your carry-on bag.
4. Switch to a better seat when the door closes.

Follow Up

After each flight, verify that the correct information appears on your credit card and frequent flyer statements. After spending the time and energy to get the lowest airfare, it would be unfortunate to be charged more; so confirm that the correct airfare appears on your credit card statement. If charged the wrong amount, call the credit card company instead of the airline or travel agent.

Consumers must notify the credit card company within 60 days of a disputed charge appearing on their statement. The company will contact the merchant (airline or travel agent) and try to correct the problem. Consumers that try to resolve the problem with the merchant are liable for the higher amount if the merchant stalls for two months. Ask the company if the dispute request must be written.

Verify that your frequent flyer statement lists all points and bonuses. Some frequent flyer programs have automated systems to check account balances. **Appendix A** lists telephone numbers for the frequent flyer programs of the ten largest U.S. airlines. Members can call an automated phone line, list recently issued points, and request credit for missing flights. Most programs update accounts within one business day of flights and allow agents to update accounts when a flight is not posted (upon request).

All frequent flyer programs require written evidence in order to issue missing points that cannot be corrected by telephone. Therefore, it is important to keep flight coupons, ticket stubs, and boarding passes until all points appear on your statement. Frequent flyer statements are not timely, either. An actual statement received on May 15 was for the period ending March 27, a delay of almost 50 days. It is inconvenient to keep your flight documents that long, especially if you fly much, but you should to insure that you receive all the points you earned.

Send complaints and compliments to appropriate parties. It is a nice gesture to send a note to the airline complimenting any personnel that helped make your flight more comfortable. If your travel agent found a great fare, send a thank you note or small gift. See **When Things Go Wrong** in this chapter for instructions about effectively filing complaints.

Figure 5.4
McCool Rule: Following Up Flights

1. Confirm price on credit card statement
2. Check automated system for posting of frequent flyer points. Later, double-check frequent flyer statement.
3. Request issuance of missing points and bonuses.
4. Send complaint and compliment letters, when necessary.

Scams

Scam, a fraudulent scheme, especially for quickly making money.

Travel Scam, a travel service sold by a fraudulent company or person. The bogus travel offering is either nonexistent or overpriced—"worthless" or "worth less."

Scam Examples

Disreputable companies and individuals cheat U.S. consumers out of $100 billion each year, according to the Federal Trade Commission (FTC). One out of every seven fraud cases involves travel, says Nolo Press. Most travel scams are conducted through the mail or by telephone. Many victims respond to a "special deal" and are subsequently cheated. Consumers can save lots of money by simply rejecting travel scams.

Scrutinize all aspects of potential travel offers, especially unbelievable deals. For example, find out if you must buy anything to get free or very cheap airfares. One common scam—free airfare certificates to popular destinations, including Hawaii and Orlando—requires the purchase of seven or more nights of overpriced lodging. For such deals, compare the typical price for flights and lodging to the deal price. Usually trips with incredible free flights cost more than similar trips with normal airfares.

Some companies offer (aggressively) to come to your home or office to pick up payment for their product. Their main objective is to get your money before you can change your mind. Do not ever feel pressured into making a decision. Tell the company you want to think about the offer; ask for a telephone number to call the next day. If you are further pressured into making a decision or not given contact information say, "No, thank you." Particularly avoid offers requiring payment of cash, check, or money order; credit card purchases are protected from fraud.

Legitimate contests do not require winners to pay anything to collect a prize. Some scams require payment of "prepaid taxes" or "shipping and handling" fees to get an unbelievable "free vacation." Victims, however, pay the fee and never receive anything.

One telephone scam is taking calls to toll-free telephone numbers (prefix of 800, 888, 877, 866, or 855) and transferring them to expensive (700, 900, or 976 prefix) or international (011 or 809 prefix) numbers. The good news is that this sneaky transfer cannot occur without the customer's authorization. Unfortunately, scam artists are clever, persistent, and able to entice consumers to ignore common sense in order to claim an "unbelievable" travel deal.

Another telephone scam has a customer call a toll-free telephone number and a salesperson calls back COLLECT. Reject collect calls from them or any unknown party. For more information about telephone scams, contact your telephone service provider, long-distance carrier, or Outfox Phone Fraud (800-968-8369, < gnat.net/outfox >). The best solution is to not respond to unsolicited offers.

Before making any travel purchase, ask detailed questions and get everything in writing. Legitimate companies will provide clients with documentation about travel offerings and answers to any questions. Scam artists usually deflect questions and simply try to get your money.

A different type of travel scam targets potential travel agents. Card mills sell a "travel agent card" entitling the bearer to free travel. The card usually costs $495 but is useless when presented to airlines and other travel suppliers. The $495 price is deliberately set to avoid FTC rules. Companies must register with the FTC when they charge over $500 and most scams are for products less than that. Incidentally, travel agents do not travel free whenever they want (see **Travel Agents** in Chapter 2).

Avoiding Scams

Apparently legitimate offers not fitting the above examples can still be scams. Keep in mind that "too good to be true" travel offers probably are! The following steps can assure that you will not be a travel scam victim.

- Use only certified travel professionals. Make sure that any potential travel agent or supplier is an ASTA (American Society of Travel Agents) member and has IATAN (International Airlines Travel Agent Network) identification. Many states have an agency that certifies and registers sellers of travel products and services.

- Ignore unsolicited offers. Telephone calls, e-mails, or letters offering a trip at an unbelievable price are usually scams; do not respond to them. Avoid telemarketers saying you have been "awarded" a vacation trip.

- Until you are completely comfortable with all aspects of a trip, do not release personal information, including credit card, Social Security, bank account, or frequent flyer numbers. Be aware of all costs, penalties, and components of any travel purchase—what you must pay and what you will receive. NEVER give CREDIT CARD information over the telephone until you are absolutely comfortable with the supplier and all aspects of the travel deal.

- Avoid companies that only accept cash, money orders, or checks. Credit card companies provide protection for most purchases. Some travel companies charge extra, usually one to five percent, for credit card transactions; the fee is sometimes disguised as a cash discount. Paying a surcharge to use a credit card is better than losing cash to an unscrupulous vendor.

- Avoid any travel deal with no set dates. Since credit card disputes can only be filed within 60 days, many scams are for trips more than two months away. When you try to book the trip, the company is no longer in business. If a company cannot provide specific dates of travel, then say, "No, thank you," and avoid the offer.

- Do not make a hurried decision. Avoid high-pressure tactics and take time to think about your purchase. Ask for a telephone number and manager's name to call for more information or when you have reached a decision. Most disreputable companies will not provide address, telephone, or personnel information.

- Get details in writing before making a payment. Find out the total price of any travel deal, including all fees and charges, cancellation and change penalties, and all components. Ask the vendor to mail or fax details about the trip. NEVER give a deposit without seeing and agreeing to all aspects of the travel offer.

- Never call telephone numbers with a 700 or 900 prefix to reach travel suppliers. Discard correspondence indicating that you must call a specific telephone number within a certain time period to claim an unbelievable travel offer.

- Avoid travel deals with any uncertain aspect. For example, scam companies often sell flights on a "major carrier," or with open dates. Asking which airline often uncovers the scam because the vendor cannot name a specific airline. Ask about every detail of a travel offer to determine its authenticity.

- Contact the Better Business Bureau (BBB) to check if complaints have been filed against any travel company. The BBB also resolves disputes between consumers and companies. Contact information for the BBB is listed in the *Yellow Pages* under Consumer Agencies, the *White Pages* under Better Business Bureau, and **Appendix C**.

Conquering Scams

You fell for a travel scam before knowing the signs or even after following the above steps. What should you do next?

Any victim of a scam should immediately try to stop payment to the vendor. If you wrote a check, ask the bank to stop the payment; the charge is about $10. A stop payment process is valid for one year and you may have to repeat the process a year later. If the scam was for a significant amount of money, then stopping the payment a couple of times can be worthwhile. For a credit card payment, call your credit card company and ask if they can stop the payment to the vendor. Cash or money order payments are rarely recovered; hopefully it was not much.

After preventing the vendor from getting paid, you should report them to local, state, and national consumer protection groups. The local and state agencies should be for their location, not yours. Sometimes it requires research to find their location. Examples of each group are listed below. **Appendix C** lists contact information for the national organizations.

Local

Better Business Bureau
Chamber of Commerce
District Attorney

State

Attorney General's Office
Consumer Affairs/Protection Office
Licensing Board (some states)

National

Better Business Bureau
Department of Transportation
Federal Communications Commission
Federal Trade Commission
National Consumer League
U.S. Postal Service

Figure 5.5
McCool Jewel: State Licensing Boards

Many states, including California and Florida, have a licensing board that certify and monitor travel vendors. Anyone selling travel products or services to consumers within the state must register with the licensing board.

When Things Go Wrong

Problems occur no matter how well trips are planned. Flights are canceled or delayed, seats are assigned to two passengers, and traffic jams cause people to miss flights.

When something goes wrong, talk to the right person and, if not your fault, ask for a specific resolution. The person listening to your complaint rarely caused the problem but usually is the only one that can help. Treat the person pleasantly because you want their assistance.

For problems such as a lengthy delay or canceled flight, call the airline's reservation telephone number instead of speaking with a person assigned to deal with the problem. Customer service agents at the airport are overwhelmed with disgruntled passengers and you will usually get quicker resolution when calling the airline. **Appendix A** lists contact information for the ten largest U.S. airlines.

For in-flight problems, talk to a flight attendant and try to reach a mutually beneficial agreement. For instance, ask for another seat if yours is broken or if unruly passengers are nearby. When a resolution cannot be reached—like the flight is full or nobody wants to switch seats—then record as many details as possible. Ask flight staff and some passengers to verify with their signatures. Witnesses, flight details, and other evidence help support your case.

If a problem cannot be resolved during the flight, then speak with customer service staff at the arrival airport. Even if they cannot offer an adequate resolution, they can at least provide the name and contact information to send your complaint.

However, the next step should be to call the airline's reservation telephone number. Call as soon as you can, explain the problem, list resolution attempts, and suggest a resolution. The agent will probably tell you to send a letter to customer service, but it does not hurt to try this step; others have been successful in solving problems by calling customer service.

Problems that cannot be resolved during the flight or by customer service staff by telephone will require written correspondence. This is where notes, evidence, and witnesses will be particularly useful. Compose a letter listing your version of the problem, appropriate details, flight staff and passenger witnesses, attempts at resolution, and reasons for unresolved status. Recommend specific compensation, such as cash refund, frequent flyer points, future travel voucher, or First Class upgrade certificate. Include copies of supporting documentation, such as boarding passes, credit card statement, frequent flyer statement, previously submitted letters, received responses, and receipts for meals, hotels, or clothing (if luggage was lost, for example).

Figure 5.6
McCool Rule: Writing Letters to Resolve Conflicts

1. Submit a Brief Explanation of Problem
2. Include Copies of Supporting Documentation
3. List Assistance Already Received
4. Recommend a Resolution

Figure 5.7
McCool Rule: Who to Contact to Resolve Problems (and the Contact Method)

1. Agents at the Scene (In-Person)
2. Agents at the Arrival Airport (In-Person)
3. Agents by Telephone (Telephone)
4. Airline's Customer Service Department (Letter, E-mail, or Telephone)
5. Airline Senior Employee (Letter, E-mail, Telephone)
6. Repeat Step 5, If Necessary (Letter, E-mail, Telephone)
7. U.S. Department of Transportation (Letter, E-mail, Telephone)

Airlines usually respond to a written complaint with a form letter. To get a satisfactory resolution it may help to send follow-up correspondence to the Vice President of Marketing or the President, in addition to the customer service department.

If there is no reasonable resolution after the second reply, then send a complaint letter to the Department of Transportation; their contact information is listed in **Appendix C**. In each follow-up correspondence, note previous attempts to reach resolution, dates of letters sent, and responses received. Keep copies of evidence and a log of correspondence.

Figure 5.8 shows a sample complaint letter. Note that it is addressed to a specific person. **Appendix A** lists the address and person for the ten largest U.S. airlines. The information is accurate as of the publication date but verify through the reservation number. Complaint letters can also be sent to many airlines through their Web sites.

Some typical problems and possible solutions:

Problem	Solution
delayed flight/ missed connection	• complimentary phone call • meal voucher • frequent flyer club pass • inconvenience voucher
canceled flight	• confirmed seat on next flight • confirmed seat on another airline • complimentary phone call • hotel or meal vouchers
overbooked flight	• First Class upgrade • free travel certificate (bumped)
double-booked seat assignment	• First Class upgrade • inconvenience voucher
lost reservation	• First Class upgrade • inconvenience voucher
delayed baggage	• inconvenience voucher • complimentary delivery
lost baggage	• cash compensation • free travel certificate

Figure 5.8
McCool Jewel:
Sample Complaint Letter

Joseph T. Flyer
12345 Second Avenue
Middletown, ST 99999-1234

XYZ Airlines
Post Office Box 1234
Kingsville, ST 33333-7575

March 4, 2001

Dear <<specific person's name (from **Appendix A**)>>,

On March 1, 2001, I was a passenger on flight 1234 from Kennedy airport to Los Angeles. I redeemed 20,000 frequent flyer points to upgrade to a First Class seat. However, a couple of problems made me wish I had kept my Coach Class seat and not waste the points.

First, the seat did not recline. If I stayed in Coach Class, I would have likely sat in an emergency row seat with extra legroom. The First Class flight attendant, Mary Williams, told me the seat was reported broken but "must not have been repaired." Second, there were not enough First Class meals and I was given a standard Coach Class meal. Had I stayed in Coach Class, I would have received a seafood meal. Ms. Williams said the airline miscalculated the number of passengers and did not have enough First Class meals.

There were no other seats to switch to, because the flight was overbooked. Attached is a note with signatures from several passengers and Ms. Williams confirming these problems.

As a long-time patron and preferred frequent flyer (over 30 flights a year), I realize this was an isolated incident. Please credit my account with the 20,000 points that I redeemed for this First Class upgrade. Thank you for your attention and assistance. I look forward to many more excellent flights with XYZ Airlines.

Sincerely,
Joe Flyer
(123) 456-7890
FF Number: 123456789

The following abridged steps from *Trouble-Free Travel*[5] show how to "Negotiate in Person When a Problem Arises."

1. Talk to the Right Person

   If your flight is canceled, it does not help to talk to a baggage handler. He might refer you to a customer service agent or may not respond at all. You should start by contacting a customer service agent.

2. The Regular Customer Advantage

   It is much more expensive for any company to attract a new customer than retain an existing one. Explaining that you enjoy flying with the airline but experienced a problem should get the attention of the management.

3. Focus on the Solution, Not the Blame

   Determine what is reasonable compensation and try to reach a settlement. Do not pursue the cause of the problem or who was at fault. Instead, focus on getting reimbursed for your inconvenience.

4. Stay Flexible

   Do not be so focused on a specific solution that you let a better one pass. You might expect a $100 travel voucher as a settlement but the airline offers 10,000 frequent flyer points. The points are worth $200, so you should accept their counteroffer.

---

[5] *Trouble-Free Travel: ... And What to Do When Things Go Wrong*, by Stephen D. Colwell and Ann R. Shulman (Nolo Press), 2nd Edition (September 1998).

5. Consider Leaving if You are Still Not Happy

    If negotiations fail or no acceptable solutions have been offered, then continue with the contact list (**Figure 5.7**). For a broken seat, first try to get reseated. If that does not work, then try to resolve with the agents at the arrival airport. Next step is to contact Customer Relations. Your case is strengthened by not accepting an unreasonable solution.

Trouble-Free Travel suggests that consumers write a Solution Letter™—similar to the description of a complaint letter a few pages earlier—when unable to resolve a problem in person. I highly recommend this book, which is entirely devoted to resolving travel problems.

Here are three examples of flight problems with solutions.

Example 1

A Miami-to-Houston-to-Los Angeles flight was canceled while I was checking in for it. The incoming flight was very late, enough to cause the Miami-to-Houston flight to miss the Houston-to-Los Angeles connection. The airline gave Miami-to-Los Angeles passengers a choice: take the two flights the next morning –OR– fly to Houston, stay overnight (passenger's cost), and fly to Los Angeles the next morning.

I did not like either option and requested a flight on another airline. The agent said no. I insisted, saying that I expected to be in Los Angeles that night, did not check any baggage, and could easily transfer to another airline. The agent still said no. I asked to speak with a supervisor. One walked by, listened to my case, and eventually placed me on an another airline's flight.

While my ticket was being reissued, I noticed other passengers were choosing to fly only to Houston or come back the next day. I was surprised that they were not more assertive.

Example 2

For a trip to Hawaii, I saved $500 by flying on a major airline to Honolulu and buying a separate interisland flight to Kona. The major airline called around 9:00 P.M., 12 hours before the flight, to tell me that the Honolulu flight was canceled. Since that flight was to an intermediate airport (Honolulu), I asked if they could rebook me to my final destination (Kona). The airline agent put me on the Kona flight—the one that cost $500 more—which left about the same time as the canceled flight was scheduled to leave.

The next morning, there were long lines at the airport, since most Honolulu passengers had to be reticketed. I was fortunate that the airline called, but resourceful to suggest a satisfactory solution for the airline and myself. Passengers confirming the flight before leaving for the airport would have learned of the cancellation and been able to reschedule by phone.

Example 3

I used frequent flyer mileage to upgrade to First Class on a one-way flight with a connection. On the first leg, my seat was broken; it would not recline. I requested a different First Class seat but there were none available. On the second leg, there were not enough First Class meals. I wrote a letter to the customer service department expressing dissatisfaction with the situation and asked for a reimbursement of the points. The airline instead sent a First Class upgrade certificate valid for any round-trip flight, which I accepted.

Airlines realize that problems occur and are willing to help passengers that are flexible, resourceful, and pleasantly assertive. I learned to state my case, pleasantly and assertively, and expect resolution for troublesome situations.

Weather Delay

The best advice for any delayed flight—whether you are trapped on the plane or in the airport terminal—is to read, catch up on correspondence, or whatever else you can do to pass idle time. Hopefully you brought along books to read, postcards or letters to write, or expense reports to complete.

It is incredibly frustrating to be trapped on an airplane that does not move, especially for an indefinite amount of time. One time I was on a plane that sat on the runway for almost three hours—and I know that there have been much longer delays! After reading the airline's magazine, gift guide, and safety info card several times, and doing the crossword puzzles (that month's issue had two), there was nothing else for me to do.

That is, nothing to do except make the best of the situation. Once an airplane leaves the gate (pushes back), passengers and crew cannot leave. You may or may not catch your connecting flight, so just try and pass the time. For weather delays, the airline is not to blame, so do not get angry with the flight crew.

Figure 5.9
McCool Jewel: Countering Weather Delays

If you have a choice, it is usually better to take the earliest flight of the day. When flights are delayed due to weather, there is a boomerang effect for the rest of the day. That is, as the day progresses, the length of delay increases.

One exception is Monterey, California. For part of the year, morning flights (departures and arrivals) are regularly delayed or canceled until the fog burns off. FAA requires visibility of a quarter mile, and it is sometimes after noon when the fog clears in Monterey. A 6:30 A.M. flight can be delayed for six hours.

Figure 5.10
McCool Jewel: Weather Delay Information

< www.fly.FAA.gov > displays real-time, up-to-date weather delay information for major U.S. airports. Always verify a flight's status with the airline, however.

Mechanical Delay

Flights can have short delays, up to an hour, for minor mechanical repairs. A part may have to be delivered from the shop, installed, and tested. The airplane then has to re-enter the flight control pattern (queue), which usually results in a separate delay.

Most pilots keep passengers informed when there is trouble. If a delay is unexplained, ask a flight attendant.

He or she should know what the problem is or can ask the pilot for an explanation.

For major delays—like a change of aircraft due to engine failure—passengers should seek and assess alternatives. When a major delay is announced, most passengers will use whatever resource is provided by the airline—usually a customer service person. A better strategy is to call the airline's toll-free reservation telephone number. It is listed on tickets and other places, including in-flight magazines, credit card and frequent flyer applications, and airport directories. **Appendix A** lists these numbers for the ten largest U.S. airlines. **Appendix B** covers many other airlines, including major international carriers.

If a flight will be delayed for several hours, ask if there are other flights to your destination. See about flights on other airlines when they cannot provide a reasonable alternative, even with connections. Sometimes there is no choice and you must simply wait for the airplane to depart.

Example

> I was on a flight that was delayed over an hour for mechanical reasons. The flight attendants finally let passengers leave the plane but asked us to remain in the boarding area to hear any announcements. I called the airline's reservation phone number and learned that the aircraft needed a new engine and that the flight was canceled. No other flights were available the rest of the day on any carrier. I requested a seat on the first flight the next morning. The airline also offered a hotel room and two meal vouchers. As I finished my call, I watched customer service agents go to the gate and announce the flight cancellation. The passengers rushed the counter and

it was a mob scene. I was lucky to have changed my plans when I did.

Travel Insurance

Flight insurance policies sold at the airport are rarely useful. They only pay benefits if the policyholder dies in a crash and only after other life insurance policies are processed. In addition, many travel agencies and credit card companies include free automatic flight insurance with all tickets.

Travel insurance, however, is a hedge against emergencies that could alter your travel plans. Airlines and other travel suppliers do not give refunds to passengers that cancel or change their plans. For instance, to shorten a trip after booking it, a traveler must make arrangements at additional cost. Policyholders get reimbursed for trips canceled or interrupted because of illness or death of family members or travel companions. Pre-existing health conditions are usually not covered. This type of travel insurance is called **Trip Cancellation & Interruption Insurance**.

Other types of travel insurance cover baggage delay, supplier bankruptcy, and lost, stolen, or damaged baggage. Some waive pre-existing conditions or permit cancellation for any reason, including a change of mind. Deductibles are usually $250 or $500. As with any type of insurance, amount limits paid daily and lifetime differ according to the provider. Also ask if the coverage is primary or secondary (supplementary). If the travel insurance is secondary coverage, then other insurance policies are processed first.

Allowable conditions for processing a policy typically include sickness, injury, or death. Some policies cover canceled, interrupted, or delayed trips due to weather, terrorism, war, employee strikes, or bankruptcy. If important, ask if allowable conditions include transportation, such as missing a connecting flight. Find whether the company has a 24-hour hotline and determine their definition of family member and travel companion. For example, some policies cover spouses and children but not parents and siblings.

Companies offering travel insurance include Cook & Company (800) 445-4821 < TravelCoverage.com > and Travel Guard (800) 826-1300 < Travel-Guard.com >. Less expensive travel insurance with the same or better features may be available through travel agents, credit card companies, or other organizations, such as work or alumni groups.

A great source for information about travel insurance is *The Savvy Adventure Traveler* by Ellen Dudley. The book has a great section called "Insuring Your Investment."

Major medical insurance is available for travel outside of the United States. Medicare and other medical insurance programs do not cover medical treatment outside the United States. In addition to medical emergencies, major medical insurance also covers evacuation and repatriation in case of death. Tour operators recommend that people over 65 years of age buy major medical insurance to cover all time spent abroad.

One discount ticket agent, Airline Reservations Network (888-847-7500, < 2flynow.com >), sells an Airfare Protection Plan for $11.99. Non-refundable fares up to $500 are refunded if a planholder cancels a flight because of injury or illness.

6

Keep Informed

The rules of the game constantly change and savvy consumers must stay informed. This chapter describes valuable resources, including the Internet, which can help you stay informed about changes to the airfare game. The best time to learn and use these resources is before you need to. When you must buy an airline ticket, you will then be familiar with the appropriate resources and strategies.

Books

Books are tremendous resources for learning how to get lower airfares. There are two types of travel books: guidebooks and reference books.

Guidebooks, like the *Frommers* and *Lonely Planet* series, are information sources about places. There is a guidebook for every tourist destination—from Antarctica to Europe to Sri Lanka. Guidebooks do not describe how to get lower airfares, however. They usually list airlines that fly to the destination and sometimes list sources of discounted flights, like consolidators or tour operators.

Reference books, like *Winning the Airfare Game,* discuss travel topics without regard to any specific destination. Subjects vary from general travel tips to specific topics like overcoming jet lag. Strategies for getting lower airfares can be found in many travel reference books. **Appendix H** lists some reference books that are particularly useful for getting lower airfares.

Browse through travel (and other subjects) books at bookstores and libraries. Bookstores sell the current editions of travel books while libraries may only have past versions. If a bookstore and library carry the same book, borrow it from the library. Library books can be checked out for a few weeks while books at a bookstore can only be browsed for a short period. After finding a must-have book, buy it from a bookstore and add it to your collection.

Bookstores

At bookstores, you can browse through books, magazines, and newspapers before buying them. Bookstores generally carry newer books and more travel magazines than libraries. Travel bookstores have a better selection of travel books and magazines than general bookstores and chains. The employees at travel bookstores are also more knowledgeable about resources that can help you get lower airfares. Some travel bookstores with Web sites are listed in **Appendix G**.

Figure 6.1
McCool Tool: Travel Bookstores with Catalogs

Adventurous Travel Bookstore	(800) 282-3963
Travel Books & Language Center	(800) 220-2665
Traveller's Bookstore	(800) 755-8728

Most bookstores sell newspapers from many cities, but you usually must buy a paper before looking at it. Libraries are better places to browse and read newspapers. Bookstores and libraries usually carry the same newspapers and receive them at the same time. See **Newspapers** in this chapter

Libraries

Search through the library's card catalog for subjects—such as *airfares*—or titles—like *Winning the Airfare Game.* Books about getting lower airfares and other travel topics appear in sections *910.2* and *917.3.* In addition to the general circulation bookshelves, check the Reference area.

Place a hold on any book checked out by another patron and the library will notify you when it is available. Incidentally, recommend this book and any other books that you find helpful. Libraries are more likely to buy books suggested by patrons.

Libraries are also a great place to read magazines and newspapers. Almost every library subscribes to several travel magazines and the Sunday edition of *The New York Times*. Your local library may also receive newspapers from cities that you plan to visit. Out-of-town newspapers usually arrive at libraries on Tuesday or Wednesday and previous editions are kept up to a year. See **Newspapers** in this chapter. Libraries also retain back issues of magazines for a year or two.

Most public libraries provide Internet access for research purposes. Web sites, newsgroups, and other Internet sources are great ways to learn about lower airfares. See **Internet** in this chapter for more information.

Magazines

Travel magazines can be useful for getting lower airfares. Browse magazines at bookstores or libraries before buying them. Subscribe to magazines that are particularly helpful; rates are as low as $10 a year. **Appendix H** lists some travel magazines that can help you get lower airfares.

Most articles in travel magazines are about destinations and you must diligently search for information about getting lower airfares. Not every issue of any travel magazine (except *Arthur Frommer's Budget Travel*) will have advice about saving money on air travel. However, nearly every travel magazine contains ads, discount certificates, or special fare announcements.

Non-travel magazines occasionally publish articles about lower airfares. Business publications are especially likely to print how-to articles for readers wanting to reduce travel costs. Ask a Reference Librarian for assistance in locating such articles.

Articles about getting lower airfares are also found on the Internet. Magazines and other sources publish many articles on their Web sites. Some articles are the same as in magazines, while other articles are unique to the Internet. Web sites such as < ABCNews.com > and < Trip.com > have collections of useful travel articles.

Newspapers

Many newspapers in the United States have resourceful Travel sections. Particularly good Travel sections appear in the weekend editions of the *Los Angeles Times, Miami Herald, The New York Times, San Jose Mercury News,* and *The Washington Post*. Most bookstores and libraries carry some of these and other newspapers.

Figure 6.2
McCool Jewel: Newspaper's Travel Sections

The Travel section of most major newspapers lists the lowest current airfares to several destinations.

Most Travel sections list the lowest current airfares to several destinations. *The New York Times* lists discounted and unrestricted airfares for several popular domestic and international routes. The *Miami Herald* lists the lowest available fares from Miami to several cities, including New York and Chicago. Advertisements from consolidators and other suppliers list low airfares. Occasional articles provide tips for getting lower airfares. However, nearly all articles are about destinations rather than general travel topics.

Radio and Television

Expedia, a major Internet booking engine, has a radio show that airs weekly. Archives of the show and a listing of radio stations airing it appear at < Expedia.com/daily/radio/ >.

The Savvy Traveler radio program can be heard on public radio stations across the United States on Saturday afternoons. The show offers lots of tips about all types of travel. Call (888) 728-8728 or visit < SavvyTraveler.com > to find out when the show airs in your area.

The Travel Channel is a cable television network that shows only travel programs. More information about The

Travel Channel can be found at < TravelChannel.com > or < Travel.Discovery.com >.

CNN Travel Now (< CNN.com/travel >) is a 30-minute program about destinations, travel trends, and international cuisine. It is on twice every Saturday morning.

PBS Travel Series is mainly about destinations. Check descriptions of its shows, like *Going Places* and *NOVA*, at < PBS.org >.

Telephone Directories

Use telephone directories to find travel agents, airlines, and other travel businesses. Various directories list companies and their contact information, including telephone and fax numbers, addresses, and Web sites. Local directories (*White Pages*) list businesses and telephone numbers in a specific area, such as a city or county. The *Yellow Pages* directories list businesses and telephone numbers by categories, such as Airlines or Travel Agents. A business pays a basic fee for a listing in *Yellow Pages* directories and an extra fee for color text or a large display ad. A prominent ad does not necessarily mean better service or lower prices.

Look at local and *Yellow Pages* directories for cities you plan to visit. Check with travel agents there for lower airfares. An agent at the destination may know about a charter airline offering low fares, for instance. Most libraries have local and *Yellow Pages* directories for several cities.

Toll-free telephone directories list businesses all over the United States that have toll-free telephone numbers. Like the *Yellow Pages*, toll-free directories are organized by categories, including Airlines and Travel Agents. Most libraries have at least one toll-free telephone directory, usually in the Reference area.

In addition to paper directories, most businesses are listed in Internet directories. Many search engines and portal Web sites have national White Pages (people finder) and Yellow Pages (business finder) telephone number directories. Toll-Free Directories include < Inter800.com > and < Anywho.com >. One online *Yellow Pages* Directory can be found at < YP.yahoo.com >.

Toll-Free Telephone Numbers

Toll-free telephone numbers are great tools for learning about lower airfares. Potential customers can call many airlines, travel agents, and other businesses at no cost. Call airlines to learn about the restrictions and fares for various routes. Call discount travel agents and consolidators to see if they offer lower airfares than airlines and other travel agents.

Any telephone number with a prefix of 800, 888, 877, 866, or 855 is toll-free. Toll-free telephone numbers are listed in telephone directories, newspapers, books, radio and TV ads, and other sources. **Appendix A** lists toll-free telephone numbers for the ten largest U.S. airlines. **Appendix B** lists toll-free telephone numbers for other airlines, including international carriers. Request any published toll-free telephone number by calling (800) 555-1212 (Toll-Free Directory Assistance). Each call to directory assistance (local, area code, or toll-free) costs 29 cents, after three free calls per month.

Travel Agents

Travel agents are probably the single best resource for getting lower airfares because they do it for their clients every day. Ask your travel agent questions to learn more about the air reservation process. For example, you can learn airfare restrictions and tips, such as using alternate airports or flying at different times of the day. See **Travel Agents** in Chapter 2.

Internet

Although some introductory topics appear in this section, the reader should be familiar with basic Internet functions, including using e-mail and the Web. This section discusses using the Internet specifically for getting lower airfares.

Using the Internet

To connect to the Internet, a user needs a computer, a modem, and an account with an **Internet Service Provider (ISP)**. There are many places to use the Internet if you do not have your own connection. Libraries provide free Internet access for research purposes. Many malls have kiosks where you can use the Internet for a few minutes. Low-cost Internet access is also available at CyberCafes, airports, and other locations, including *Kinko's*.

Electronic Mail (E-mail)

Electronic mail, or **e-mail**, is the most common Internet task. Nearly all ISPs allow users to send messages to any Internet address. Corresponding with others by e-mail is an effective way to learn about lower airfares. For instance, send a note to someone that wrote an article about budget travel and request additional information.

Most e-mail programs allow files to be attached to messages. E-mail **attachments** can be useful tools for getting lower airfares. For example, the author can send an e-mail attachment listing current toll-free telephone numbers for hundreds of airlines around the world. To request the current list, send a blank e-mail message to < airlinelist@lowerairfares.com >.

Mailing Lists

A **mailing list**, or **Listserv**, sends information about a particular topic by e-mail to many people. < Liszt.com > describes mailing lists (of every subject) and has instructions for joining them. Listserv messages are either sent to members as they are received or they are collected and sent all at once (**digest** mode).

Mailing lists can inform you of last-minute specials, airfare sales, new routes, airfare changes, promotions, or general air travel news. Airlines send e-mail notifications with last-minute specials on Tuesday or Wednesday each week. These last-minute flights usually leave the next Friday or Saturday and return the following Monday or Tuesday. Occasional specials apply to flights on other days. Sometimes there are international airfare specials, either last minute or for a specified time period.

Smarter Living (< SmarterLiving.com >) organizes the last-minute specials by airport. For instance, their weekly Washington, DC e-mail lists flights to and from Baltimore, Dulles, and National airports.

Appendix G lists some Web sites that send e-mail about last-minute airfare specials. Visit the appropriate Web site and follow the registration instructions. In most cases, you complete a short, simple form.

World Wide Web (WWW) and Web Sites

Besides e-mail, the most common Internet function is the **World Wide Web** (WWW) or **Web** for short. Most Web site addresses or URLs (Uniform Resource Locators) start with "http://www."

Web addresses in this book do not include the "http://www." portion; for example:

< http://www.lowerairfares.com >

is shown as

< LowerAirfares.com >.

The shortened URL (LowerAirfares.com) usually works in any Web browser. If it does not, then enter "www." before it (www.LowerAirfares.com). It does not matter whether the URL text is uppercase or lowercase; lowerairfares.com, LowerAirfares.Com, and LOWERAIRFARES.COM are interpreted the same way. Uppercase letters are used in the examples for emphasis (better readability). However, filenames in URLs are case-sensitive; < 123.com/A.htm > is different from < 123.com/a.htm >.

Search engines are one place to look for potentially useful Web sites. For many search engines, enclosing a phrase in quotes will find only the exact term, eliminating many inappropriate Web sites. Read the tips and rules for various search engines. Enter keywords like "lower airfares" and then select a Web site from the result list. **Appendix G** lists some major search engines. When you find a useful Web site, add it to your Bookmark list. To visit that Web site in the future, simply select the bookmark from the list.

Many Web sites allow users to buy airline tickets. Using booking Web sites, such as < Travelocity.com >, is similar to a travel agent using a computer reservation system; flights from many airlines are shown. Most airlines Web sites only display their own flights. In addition to booking flights, airline's Web sites have frequent flyer program information, discount fares, promotions, and general news. Other Web sites let you track current flights, find travel tips, or view the rules and restrictions for various fares. **Appendix G** lists some of the most popular booking Web sites.

One future Web site, nicknamed T2 (Orbitz.com as of June 2000), intends to give consumers a one-stop shopping experience to find the lowest airfare. Currently, consumers must visit a half-dozen Web sites to truly find the lowest airfare. Orbitz' search engine will analyze, for any route, all possible connections using all airlines, including consolidator fares, and return a list of the lowest fares. It is funded by several airlines, leading skeptics (mostly travel agents) to say that it cannot possibly benefit consumers. As of September 2000, < Orbitz.com > is scheduled to launch in the summer of 2001.

Web sites without a booking engine can still be useful. For instance, many sites display current last-minute airfares, either all of them or a subset based on search results.

> **< SmarterLiving.com > lists current last-minute specials by airport. The information is the same as sent to subscribers by e-mail (see description above in Mailing Lists). At the Web site, select the "Search Fares" feature, select an airport, and view the results.**

Using Booking Web Sites

A good strategy is to use one booking Web site for research and compare the results with at least one other Web site. For standard round-trip flight scenarios, each engine provides the same flight options and prices. Personal preferences will dictate which Web site is best. Even if you do not buy a ticket from the Web site, you will at least know that you found the lowest fare. You may decide to buy the ticket from the airline, a travel agent, or a different Web site.

Each Web site has its own set of features and not all features appear on every Web site. Some allow selection of an exact seat, while others only let you specify a window or aisle preference. Users can hold reservations at some Web sites and only buy tickets at others.

Some booking Web sites notify members about airfare changes. Users can specify routes and set price ranges. An e-mail message is sent when the price is within the range or falls below the target price. Most sites have tickers listing the lowest current fares for popular routes. Most sites also have low-fare finders that search for the lowest fares on the selected dates of travel.

Although the fares are usually the same for most round-trip flights, differences can occur for complicated scenarios and international routes. For example, prices for Washington, DC-to-Johannesburg, South Africa flights were over $2,000 when using the low fare finder from various booking sites. Most of the flights required changing airlines in London. Fares dropped to $1,000 when bypassing the automated feature and selecting specific flights.

> **Preview Travel < Reservations.com > has a feature called FareFinder that lists the current lowest fares from many airports. For example, pick LAX (Los Angeles) and the lowest fares are displayed to 57 domestic and 40 international airports. Fares that are five percent or more less than the average cost over the preceding three months are highlighted.**

> **Travelocity < Travelocity.com > has a feature called Dream Map. Type in a departure city or airport, like Los Angeles or LAX, and select an upper limit between $100 and $1,000; some places you can fly for that fare or less appears.**

Message Boards

Internet message board users are very willing to share experiences, tips, and strategies—about getting lower airfares or any other topic. Message boards can be part of Web sites or America Online content areas. Message board tips reflect actual user experiences and can be very valuable. Information from other sources is often restated announcements—fare war sales, new routes, last-minute specials, and such. For example, one might describe getting a low fare to Turkey through a foreign consolidator. Those tips are much more useful than searching through fare engines.

Figure 6.3
McCool Jewel: Internet Message Boards

Information from message boards is more valuable than from other sources because it reflects actual experiences.

Each message board discussion or topic is called a **thread**. Anyone can view and respond to other's inquiries. It is common for a thread to take on different themes than intended by the original poster. For instance, a message asks for tips on using First Class upgrade certificates. Varied responses give advice, have an "I also want to know that!" tone, or are confrontational—like "only blowhards fly in First Class." The discussion may evolve into "favorite airlines" or "restaurants to visit."

Instead of posting an unrelated message on a board, send a note directly to the appropriate person. For instance, a discount travel agent posted a response about Denmark and you want to ask advice about airfares to Asia. Send an e-mail message to the agent instead of posting a message on the board and distracting the thread.

Newsgroups

Newsgroups are similar to message boards except that they are not owned by specific Web sites or content areas; newsgroups are public. Anyone with a newsreader (included with browser software) can access newsgroups. DejaNews <deja.com/usenet> allows users to view messages and subscribe to any newsgroup. America Online users can access newsgroups through the Internet Channel or Keyword: newsgroups. Some appropriate newsgroups for getting lower airfares are listed in **Appendix G.**

Content Areas (America Online)

Information in America Online (AOL) appears in **content areas** or **channels**. The Travel Channel (Keyword: travel) is the most appropriate place for finding and sharing information about lower airfares. Travel Channel areas include Bargain Box, Independent Traveler, Resource Center, and Travel Bargains.

Other channels can contain information about finding lower airfares. Travel Services (Keyword: travel industry) in the WorkPlace Channel is designed for travel agents and other industry employees. The Reference Channel has a toll-free telephone directory and other resources.

Other areas can be found in AOL's Keyword list. To find keywords starting with "travel," access the Keyword command and type "keyword." In the subsequent window, choose the List Alphabetically option and select the "TN—TY Keywords" option. There are dozens of "travel" keywords. Repeat the process to find other keywords; for instance starting with "air" or "budget."

Figure 6.4
McCool Rule: Using the Internet

1. Search for low fares on booking Web sites
2. Register with low-fare notifier services
3. Subscribe to last-minute mailing lists
4. Participate in message board and newsgroup discussions
5. Send e-mail with specific questions to qualified sources

Netiquette

Turn off the CAPS LOCK key on your keyboard before typing messages. Typing with all CAPITAL LETTERS is the online equivalent of shouting at someone. The text is annoying and difficult to read. Many people ignore e-mails and message board postings written in all caps, because it is a sign of a novice or ignorant computer user.

To emphasize certain words, use boldface style, asterisks, all caps, or HTML tags (where allowed). Use these methods sparingly. Some examples:

Airfares are **not** guaranteed until purchased.

Airfares are *not* guaranteed until purchased.

Airfares are NOT guaranteed until purchased.

Airfares are <I>not</I> guaranteed until purchased.

In the last example, *not* appears italicized where HTML tags are used. If HTML is not recognized, then "<I>not</I>" appears—so be certain that tags are converted before you post a message. Many message boards permit simple HTML tags; ask the Webmaster if you are not sure.

Spam is unsolicited e-mail sent in bulk to many (usually thousands) people. Posting commercial or unrelated messages in newsgroups or message boards can also be considered spam. Besides being annoying and insulting, spamming is against ISP's rules and may also be illegal.

The number one reason for the Internet's popularity is the ability to quickly find necessary or desired information. Sharing information is an essential aspect of this popularity. When you discover an incredible airfare deal, post a message in an appropriate newsgroup (after making sure no one else did). Share travel tips and learn new ones in online discussions (chats and message boards). Send a thank you e-mail message to anyone helping you learn how to get lower airfares—such as someone recommending a useful Web site or replying to your message board post.

Figure 6.5
McCool Rule: Internet Etiquette or "Net"iquette

1. Turn off the CAPS LOCK key
2. Don't Spam
3. Thank others for information
4. Share information with others

Internet Safety

Protection of sensitive data is a primary concern for all Internet users. The Internet is one of the safest mediums in spite of media portrayal of it as a haven for fraud. Internet fraud is estimated at $1 loss per $1,000 in transactions (in 1999). This compares favorably with cellular telephone fraud ($20 lost per $1,000 spent). Credit card and long distance frauds are also more prevalent than Internet fraud.

Many people are comfortable giving credit card and Social Security numbers by telephone or mail, where fraud occurs more than on the Internet. Use caution in any situation and do not disclose personal or financial information until you are sure of the integrity of the other party.

Use only secure Web sites to transmit sensitive information. Secure Servers use encryption algorithms to protect user data. There are a couple of ways to determine if a Web site is secure. The browser's lower left window displays a special symbol when the Web site is secure; Netscape's browser displays a bright key logo and Internet Explorer shows a locked key. Another way to know that a Web site is secure is that the URL starts with "https" instead of "http."

Some Web sites require a user name and password (subscription). Most of the time, there is no charge to get an account (subscribe). In the near future, it may be common to pay for services that are now free. Web sites typically use subscriptions to track usage and collect statistics. Many Web sites use **cookies** to track users. Simple cookies store names, so that users can be personally greeted each visit. More complex cookies encode personal data, including credit card information.

Putting It All Together

One summer I wanted to fly to a new country, as inexpensively as possible. Someone recommended that I try a courier flight. As a result of research and good fortune, I ended up taking several flights—to South Korea, Hong Kong, Japan, Hawaii, Australia, and Florida (all from California)—AND earned 50,000 frequent flyer miles without PAYING A DIME. In fact, I was paid to fly to all of these places.

At that time, Northwest Airlines offered 5,000 bonus frequent flyer miles for each transpacific segment; a round-trip flight earned 10,000 extra points. Hong Kong was the destination that I selected, since the points—over 25,000 with the 10,000 point bonus—would be enough for a free flight. I even decided to fly to Florida later that year with the award.

IBC-Pacific offered courier flights between Los Angeles and Hong Kong on Northwest Airlines for $350. Their flights stopped in Seoul, South Korea on the way to Hong Kong and in Tokyo on the way home. Quickly, I decided that $350 for flights to Hong Kong and Florida was a great deal. Unfortunately, IBC no longer offers courier flights. After using my credit card to hold my reservation with IBC's travel agent, I called the airline, verified the itinerary, and requested a seat assignment. Being able to pay with a credit card and call the airline eased my concerns about the legitimacy of the courier operation.

Between making the reservation and the travel day, I paid for the flight, received a packet of instructions, and reconfirmed the itinerary several times. As required by the instructions, I checked in at a specific Northwest Airlines counter three hours before the scheduled departure time. The counter agent checked my passport, verified my seat assignment, and told me an IBC employee would appear soon. About 20 minutes later one showed. He gave me a manila envelope with the shipment manifest and nametags—so representatives in Seoul and Hong Kong could easily identify me.

In Seoul, I cleared Customs and met a local representative. A big relief was that I did not have to retrieve the cargo. The representative took the envelope and drove me to a downtown hotel; IBC paid for the Seoul hotel stay. I converted $20 and had dinner close to the hotel. The next day, I took a taxi to the airport, flew to Hong Kong, and met another representative. He told me to call the Hong Kong office two days before my return flight.

Eight days later, I called and was told to meet someone at the Northwest Airlines information counter 2 1/2 hours before the flight departure. That representative collected my departure tax (about $20), passport, and ticket, then checked me onto the flight. Having someone else take care of the check-in process for an international return flight is a true joy; it was one of the best benefits of the courier process. He told me that I had no duties for the return trip and left. I ate breakfast, bought a couple of duty-free items, and flew to Tokyo.

The Tokyo-to-Los Angeles flight was overbooked and I was the first passenger to volunteer to be bumped. In exchange for taking a different flight, I received a $400 check, a $600 travel voucher, and dinner at the Tokyo airport. I was concerned that being bumped would be a dereliction of my courier duties. However, since I had no duties for the return trip, my biggest risk was losing the $500 deposit. The $1,000 compensation for being bumped alleviated my fears of losing the deposit, so I let the airline bump me. About two weeks later I received my deposit.

All Northwest flights were full that day and I ended up on a mostly empty Singapore Airlines flight, with an entire row to myself. Even though I was bumped from the Tokyo-to-Los Angeles flight, I received the frequent flyer and bonus points from Northwest. In addition, I received points for the Singapore Airlines flight, which were transferred to a partner carrier's program.

The following summer, I redeemed the $600 travel voucher for a Los Angeles-to-Sydney flight with a stopover in Honolulu. The cost was $626, so I had to pay $26. I had more luck, as the Los Angeles-to-Honolulu flight was overbooked and I was again bumped. This time I *only* got a free domestic ticket—which I later used for a San Francisco-to-Miami flight—and a comfortable flight on a half-empty Delta plane. Again, I received frequent flyer points for both flights.

In total, I spent $376—$350 for the courier flight and $26 for the Australia trip—and received $400—from the bumped Tokyo-to-Los Angeles flight. I came out $24 ahead. OK, counting the $20 departure tax in Hong Kong, I only came out $4 ahead. In addition, I received frequent flyer points for all except the Florida flights. I added over 50,000 points to accounts.

Originally, I planned on getting a free flight to Florida by redeeming 25,000 points earned from the Los Angeles-to-Hong Kong courier flight. The two bumped flights gave me a free flight to Florida—from the Los Angeles-to-Honolulu flight—and 15,000 more points—from the Los Angeles-to-Sydney round-trip flight. Instead, I exchanged 40,000 Northwest points for a San Francisco-to-Europe flight. However, there were no bumping incidents, so my free flights adventure came to an end.

Appendix A
Ten Largest U.S. Airlines

Appendix A lists contact information for the ten largest airlines in the United States. The reservation telephone number is the main point of contact for each airline. Reservation agents can usually do all services, including domestic and international reservations, frequent flyer account information, flight arrival and departure, itinerary confirmation, and customer service. If not, they can transfer you or provide the correct telephone number. These (I), (A), (F), and (S) telephone numbers are direct, bypassing the main reservation (R) number.

Airline Name (CODE)
< Web Site Address >

(R)	Reservations (main number)
(I)	International Reservations
(A)	Automated Flight Information
(F)	Frequent Flyer Program
(S)	Customer Service

Alaska Airlines (AS)
< AlaskaAir.com >

(R/I/A)	(800) 252-7522
(F)	(800) 622-2680
(S)	(800) 654-5669
(S – fax)	(206) 433-3477

Ms. Valerie Svilarich
Director, Consumer Affairs
P.O. Box 68900
Seattle, WA 98168

American Airlines (AA)
< AA.com >

(R/I)	(800) 433-7300
(A)	(800) 223-5436
(F)	(800) 882-8880
(S)	(817) 967-2000
(S - fax)	(817) 967-4162

Ms. Maryanne McCabe-Cipperly
Managing Director
Consumer Relations
P.O. Box 619612 M/D 2400
DFW Airport, TX 75261-9612

America West Airlines (HP)
< AmericaWest.com >

(R/A/S)	(800) 235-9292
(I)	(800) 533-6862
(F)	(800) 247-5691
(S)	(800) 363-2542
(S)	(602) 693-3707

Ms. Jill Vicchy
Manager, Customer Relations
4000 E. Sky Harbor Blvd.
Phoenix, AZ 85034

Continental Airlines (CO)
< Continental.com >

(R)	(800) 525-0280
(I)	(800) 231-0856
(A)	(800) 784-4444
(F)	(713) 952-1630
(S)	(800) 932-2732
(S - fax)	(713) 590-2150

Ms. Judith Mensinger
Director, Customer Care
3663 N. Sam Houston Parkway
Suite 500
Houston, TX 77032

Delta Air Lines (DL)
< Delta.com >

Appendix A
Ten Largest U.S. Airlines

Delta Air Lines (DL)
< Delta.com >

(R)	(800) 221-1212
(I)	(800) 241-4141
(A)	(800) 325-1999
(F)	(800) 323-2323
(S)	(404) 715-1450
(S - fax)	(404) 715-1400

Ms. Patricia J. Robinette
Director, Consumer Affairs
Hartsfield-Atlanta Int'l Airport
Atlanta, GA 30320

Northwest Airlines (NW)
< NWA.com >

(R/F)	(800) 225-2525
(I)	(800) 447-4747
(A)	(800) 441-1818
(S)	(612) 726-2046
(S - fax)	(612) 726-0776

Ms. Cindy Scheer
Director, Customer and Sales Support
5101 Northwest Drive M/S C6590
St. Paul, MN 55111

Southwest Airlines (WN)
< Southwest.com >

(R)	(800) 435-9792
(S)	(214) 792-4223
(S - fax)	(214) 792-1611
(S - fax)	(214) 792-5099

Mr. Jim Ruppel
Director, Customer Relations
P.O. Box 36611, Love Field
Dallas, TX 75235-1611

Trans World Airlines (TW)
< TWA.com >

(R)	(800) 221-2000
(I)	(800) 892-4141
(A)	(800) 893-5436
(F)	(800) 325-4815
(S)	(314) 589-3600
(S)	(610) 631-5280

Ms. Susan Ahl
Staff VP, Customer Relations
1415 Olive Street, Suite 100
St. Louis, MO 63103

United Airlines (UA)
< UAL.com >

(R)	(800) 241-6522
(I)	(800) 538-2929
(A)	(800) 824-6200
(F)	(800) 421-4655
(S)	(847) 700-6796
(S - fax)	(847) 700-2214

Ms. Denise Harvill
Director, Customer Relations
P.O. Box 66100
Chicago, IL 60666

US Airways (US)
< USAirways.com >

(R)	(800) 428-4322
(I)	(800) 622-1015
(A)	(800) 943-5436
(F)	(800) 872-4738
(S)	(336) 661-0061
(S - fax)	(336) 661-8031

Ms. Deborah Thompson
Director, Consumer Affairs
P.O. Box 1501
Winston-Salem, NC 27102-1501

Appendix B
Other Airlines

Regional U.S. Airlines

AirTran Airways (FL)	(800) 247-8726	< AirTran.com >
Aloha Airlines (AQ)	(800) 367-5250	< AlohaAir.com >
American Trans Air (TZ)	(800) 435-9282	< ATA.com >
Continental Micronesia (CS)	(800) 214-1469	< FlyMicronesia.com >
Frontier Airlines (F9)	(800) 432-1359	< Frontierairlines.com >
Hawaiian Airlines (HA)	(800) 367-5320	< HawaiianAir.com >
Horizon Airlines (AW)	(800) 547-9308	< HorizonAir.com >
Legend Airlines (LC)	(877) 359-5343	< LegendAirlines.com >
Mahalo Air (8M)	(800) 462-4256	
Markair (BF)	(800) 627-5247	
Martinair (MP)	(800) 366-4655	< MartinairUSA.com >
* Mesa Airlines (YV)	(800) 637-2247	< Mesa-Air.com >
Midway Airlines (JI)	(800) 446-4392	< MidwayAir.com >
Midwest Express (YX)	(800) 452-2022	< MidwestExpress.com >
National Airlines (5J)	(888) 757-5387	< NationalAirlines.com >
Nations Air Express (N5)	(800) 248-9538	< NationsAir.com >
Reeve Aleutian Airways (RV)	(800) 544-2248	< ReeveAir.com >
Spirit Airlines (NK)	(800) 772-7117	< SpiritAir.com >
Sun Country Airlines (SY)	(800) 752-1218	< Suncountry.com >
Tower Air (FF)	(800) 221-2500	< TowerAir.com >
Vanguard Airlines (NJ)	(800) 826-4827	< FlyVanguard.com >

* Most flights on Mesa Airlines can be reserved through their affiliates: American West Express, United Express, and USAirways Express.

International Airlines

Aer Lingus (EI)	(800) 223-6537	< AerLingus.ie >
Aero Peru (PL)	(800) 777-7717	< AeroPeru.usa.com >
Aeroflot (SU)	(800) 995-5555	< Aeroflot.org >
Aerolineas Argentinas (AR)	(800) 333-0276	< Aerolineas.com.ar >
Aeromexico (AM)	(800) 237-6639	< Aeromexico.com >
Air Canada (AC)	(800) 776-3000	< AirCanada.ca >
Air China (CA)	(800) 982-8802	< AirChina.com >
Air France (AF)	(800) 237-2747	< AirFrance.fr >
Air India (AI)	(800) 223-2250	< AirIndia.com >
Air Jamaica (JM)	(800) 523-5585	< AirJamaica.com >
Air New Zealand (NZ)	(800) 262-1234	< AirNZ.com >
Alitalia (AZ)	(800) 223-5730	< Alitalia.it >

Appendix B
Other Airlines

Airline	Phone	Website
All Nippon Airways (NH)	(800) 235-9262	< ANA.co.jp/eng >
Ansett Airlines (AN)	(800) 366-1300	< Ansett.com.au >
Asiana Airlines (OZ)	(800) 227-4262	< Asiana.co.kr/english >
Austrian Airlines (OS)	(800) 843-0002	< AUA.com >
Avianca (AV)	(800) 284-2622	< Avianca.com.co >
British Airways (BA)	(800) 247-9297	< British-Airways.com >
British Midland (BD)	(800) 788-0555	< IFlyBritishMidland.com >
BWIA West Indies Air (BW)	(800) 538-2942	< BWee.com >
Canadian Airlines (CP)	(800) 426-7000	< CndAir.ca >
Cathay Pacific Airways (CX)	(800) 233-2742	< Cathay-usa.com >
Cayman Airways (KX)	(800) 422-9626	< Cayman.com.ky/com/cal >
China Airlines (CI)	(800) 227-5118	< China-Airlines.com >
China Southern (CZ)	(888) 388-8988	< CS-air.com/en >
City Bird (HZ)	(888) 248-9247	< CityBird.com >
Egyptair (MS)	(800) 334-6787	< Egyptair.com.eg >*
El Al Israel Airlines (LY)	(800) 223-6700	< ElAl.co.il >
Ethiopian Airlines (ET)	(877) 389-6753	< EthiopianAirlines.com>
EVA Airways (BR)	(800) 695-1188	< EVAAir.com.tw >
Finnair (AY)	(800) 950-5000	< us.Finnair.com >
Garuda Indonesia (GA)	(800) 342-7832	< Garuda.co.id >
Iberia (IB)	(800) 772-4642	< Iberia.com/ingles >
Icelandair (FI)	(800) 223-5500	< Icelandair.is >
Japan Airlines (JL)	(800) 525-3663	< JAL.co.jp >
Kenya Airways (KQ)	(800) 343-2506	< KenyaAirways.co.uk >
KLM Royal Dutch Air (KL)	(800) 374-7747	< KLM.com >
Korean Air (KE)	(800) 438-5000	< KoreanAir.com >
Kuwait Airways (KU)	(800) 458-9248	< KuwaitAir.de >
LACSA (LR)	(800) 225-2272	< CentralAmerica.com/cr/lacsa >
LAN Chile (LA)	(800) 735-5526	< LANChile.com >
Lauda Air	(800) 588-8399	< LaudaAir.com >
LOT Polish (LO)	(800) 223-0593	< LOT.com/english >
LTU Int'l Airways (LT)	(800) 888-0200	< LTU.com >
Luthansa (LH)	(800) 645-3800	< Lufthansa-usa.com >
Malaysia Airlines (MH)	(800) 421-8641	< Malaysia-Airlines.com >
Malev Airlines (MA)	(800) 262-5380	< Malev.hu >
Mexicana Airlines (MX)	(800) 531-7921	< Mexicana.com >

Appendix B
Other Airlines

Olympic Airways (OA)	(800) 223-1226	< Olympic-Airways.gr >
Pakistan Int'l Airlines (PK)	(800) 221-6024	< FlyPIA.com >
Philippine Airlines (PR)	(800) 435-9725	< PhilippineAir.com >
Qantas Airways (QF)	(800) 227-4500	< Qantas.com >
Royal Air Maroc (AT)	(800) 344-6726	< RoyalAirMaroc.com >
Royal Jordanian (RJ)	(800) 223-0470	< RJA.com.jo >
Sabena (SN)	(800) 955-5000	< Sabena.com >
SAS Scandinavian Air (SK)	(800) 221-2350	< SAS.se >
Saudi Arabian Airlines (SV)	(800) 472-8342	< SaudiAirlines.com >
Singapore Air (SQ)	(800) 742-3333	< SingaporeAir.com >
South African Airways (SA)	(800) 722-9675	< SAA.co.za/saa >
Spanair (JK)	(888) 545-5757	< Spanair.com >
Swissair (SR)	(800) 221-4750	< Swissair.com >
TACA Int'l Airlines (TA)	(800) 535-8780	< GrupoTACA.com >
TAP Air Portugal (TP)	(800) 221-7370	< TAP-AirPortugal.pt >
Thai Airways (TG)	(800) 426-5204	< ThaiAir.com >
Transbrasil (TR)	(800) 872-3153	< TransBrasil.com.br >
Tyrolean Airways		< Tyrolean.at >
Varig Brazilian Airlines (RG)	(800) 468-2744	< Varig.com.br >
VASP Brazilian Airlines (VP)	(800) 433-0444	< VASP.com.br >
Virgin Atlantic Airways (VS)	(800) 862-8621	< Fly.Virgin.com >

* Almost every business (especially airlines) has a Web site. Typing the name of the company and "dot com"—such as Egyptair.com—will often go to its Home page. The Web sites for many international airlines are hosted in their country. For instance, < Egyptair.com.eg > is the home page for Egyptair. < EgyptAir.com > is an unrelated Web site for an air quality company. Other airlines will mirror their Web sites on the .com domain. Swissair, for example, can be found at < SwissAir.ch > and < SwissAir.com >. Airline Web sites not listed can be found through a Search Engine or a Web site that lists airlines; examples of each are included in Appendix G.

To find a telephone number for an airline not listed, call Toll-Free Directory Assistance at (800) 555-1212. To find the Web site for an airline not listed, visit one of the Web sites listed in **Appendix G** (Web Sites with Airline Lists).

Appendix C
Consumer Organizations

Air Transport Association
1301 Pennsylvania Ave., NW
Suite 1100
Washington, DC 20004-1707
(202) 626-4000
< Air-transport.org >
- Safety concerns

American Society of Travel Agents
Consumer Affairs Department
1101 King Street
Alexandria, VA 22314
(703) 739-ASTA
(703) 684-8319 (fax)
< ASTAnet.com/pub >
- Travel agent certification, resolves consumer-agent disputes

Pamphlet: Avoiding Travel Problems

Aviation Consumer Action Project
529 14th Street, NW
Suite 1265
Washington, DC 20045
(202) 638-4000
< ACAP1971.org >
- Safety & rights

Better Business Bureau
4200 Wilson Blvd. Suite 800
Arlington, VA 22203-1838
(703) 276-0100
< BBB.org >
- Online booklets about Consolidators, Using Travel Agents, Travel Packages, Lost Luggage, and more.

Federal Aviation Administration
Community & Liaison Division
APA-400
800 Independence Avenue, SW
Washington, DC 20591
(800) 322-7873 (consumer hotline)
(800) 255-1111 (safety hotline)
< FAA.gov/passinfo.htm >
- Air safety

Federal Communications Commission
Consumer Information Bureau
445 12th Street, SW
Washington, DC 20554
(888) 225-5322 (CALL-FCC)
(202) 418-0191
(202) 418-0232 (fax)
< FCC.gov/cib >
- Contact them about fraudulent radio or television ads, or telemarketing or telephone scams

Federal Trade Commission
Consumer Response Center
Federal Trade Commission
600 Pennsylvania Avenue, NW
Washington, DC 20580
(877) 382-4357
(202) 326-2222
(202) 326-3238
(202) 326-2050 (fax)
< FTC.gov/ftc/consumer.htm >
- Booklets: Telemarketing Travel Fraud, Car Rental, or Timeshares

Appendix C
Consumer Organizations

Florida Department of Agriculture and Consumer Services
Division of Consumer Services
407 South Calhoun Street
Mayo Building
Tallahassee, Florida 32399-0800
(800) 435-7352 (HELP-FLA)
(850) 488-2221
< doacs.state.fl.us/~cs >
< 800helpfla.com >
- Verify that a company is registered or has had no complaints filed against. In Florida, consumers can cancel a vacation purchase within 30 days.
- Check for a similar organization in other states.

National Fraud Information Center
c/o National Consumers League
1701 K Street, NW
Suite 1200
Washington, DC 20005
(800) 835-3323
(800) 876-7060
(202) 835-0747 (fax)
< Fraud.org >
- Submit inquiries about questionable companies
- Request list of questions to ask potential scam companies

U.S. Department of Transportation
Aviation Consumer Protection Division (ACPD)
400 Seventh Street, SW
Room 4107, C-75
Washington, DC 20590
(800) 221-0673[1] (travel advisory)
(202) 755-2220
(202) 366-2220 (ACPD)
(202) 366-7907 (fax)
< DOT.gov/airconsumer >

U.S. Postal Service
Inspection Services
475 L'Enfant Plaza, SW
Washington, DC 20260
(202) 268-4267
(202) 268-4563 (fax)
< USPS.gov >
- Report any company sending a scam through the U.S. mail.

U.S. Tour Operators Association
324 Madison Avenue
Suite 1522
New York, NY 10173
(212) 599-6599
(212) 599-6744 (fax)
< USTOA.com >
- Contact USTOA if you have a problem with a package deal.

---

[1] Press "1" to transfer to the State Department advisory line. Direct number is (202) 647-5225.

Appendix D
Courier Resources

Company Name	Telephone #	Flights From:
Courier Travel Service	(516) 763-6898	New York
Discount Travel Int'l	(212) 362-3636	New York, Miami
East-West Express	(718) 656-6242	New York
Halbart Express	(718) 656-8189	New York, Miami, Boston
Halbart Express	(703) 318-6520	Washington, DC (Dulles)
Jupiter Air	(310) 670-5123	Los Angeles
Jupiter Air	(415) 697-1773	San Francisco
Midnight Express	(310) 330-7096	Los Angeles
* Now Voyager	(212) 431-1616	New York, Miami, Houston
UTL	(415) 583-5074	San Francisco
Way to Go	(213) 466-1126	Los Angeles, San Francisco

* Recording of courier and non-courier flights is updated daily.

Membership Groups:

Air Courier Association	(800) 282-1202	None
IAATC	(561) 582-8320	None
Worldwide Courier Assoc.	(800) 780-4359	None

Web Sites

< AirCourier.org >	Air Courier Association
< AirCour.org >	Air Cour. Conference of America
< Courier.org >	Int'l Assoc. of Air Travel Couriers
< JupiterAir.com/serv02.htm >	Jupiter Air
< NowVoyagerTravel.com >	Now Voyager
< Wallstech.com >	Worldwide Courier Association

Other Sources

See **Appendix H** for books about courier air travel.
Get recommendations from Internet message boards and newsgroups.
See *Air Travel* or *Tickets* categories in classified sections of major newspapers.

Appendix E
Round the World Resources

Company Name < Web Address >	Toll-Free Telephone #	Location
Air Brokers International < AirBrokers.com >	(800) 883-3273	San Francisco, CA
Around the World Travel < JustFares.com > and < NetFare.net >	(800) 766-3601	Seattle, WA
DIA International Travel < DIATravel.com >	(800) 342-8258	Washington, DC
High Adventure Travel < HighAdv.com > and < AirTreks.com >	(800) 350-0612	Palo Alto, CA
Scan the World < ScanTheWorld.com >	(800) 775-0200	Palo Alto, CA
Ticket Planet < TicketPlanet.com >	(800) 799-8888	San Francisco, CA
World Traveller's Club < Around-The-World.com >	(800) 693-0411	San Francisco, CA

Other Sources

Round-The-World Travel Guide.
< Travel-Library.com/rtw/html/FAQ.html >
One Year Off. Cohen, David Elliott. Simon & Schuster.
The Practical Nomad. Hasbrouck, Edward. Moon Travel Handbooks.
< Moon.com/practical_nomad >.
< LowerAirfares.com/RTW >

Appendix F
Charter and Consolidator Resources

Some companies that issue different types of tickets appear in more than one Appendix. *Air Brokers International,* for instance, sells Charter, Consolidator, and Round the World (RTW) tickets; they are listed in three places. Hundreds of travel agencies sell consolidator tickets but only about 25 are listed. *Fly Cheap!* (see **Appendix H**) has an extensive listing of consolidators, sorted by location.

Charter Companies – That Sell Only to Travel Agents

Air-Tech	(212) 219-7000	< AirTech.com >
Jetset Tours	(800) 638-3273	< JetsetTours.com >
* Travac	(800) 872-8800	< Travac.com >
UniTravel	(800) 325-2222	< UniTravel.com >

* Travac's Web site for consumers is < TheTravelSite.com >.

Charter Companies – That Sell to Consumers

City Bird	(888) 248-9247	< CityBird.com >
Council Travel	(800) 226-8624	< CouncilTravel.com >
Fantasy Holidays	(800) 645-2555	< FantasyHolidays.com >
GWV International	(800) 225-5498	< GWVtravel.com >
Homeric Tours	(800) 223-5570	< HomericTours.com >
Martinair	(800) 366-4655	< MartinairUSA.com >
New Frontiers USA	(800) 366-6387	< NewFrontiers.com >
SunTrips	(800) 786-8747	< SunTrips.com >
Travel Charter International	(800) 521-5267	< TravelCharter.com >

Consolidators

1travel.com	(800) 929-2523	< OneTravel.com >
Air Brokers Int'l	(800) 883-3273	< AirBrokers.com >
Air Travel Discounts	(888) 888-2621	< AirTravelDiscounts.com >
Amer. Passenger Consldtrs.	(800) 526-2447	< APC-consolidators.com >
Air Hitch - California	(800) 834-9192	< AirHitch.org >
Air Hitch – New York	(800) 326-2009	< AirHitch.org >
Cheap Tickets	(800) 377-1000	< CheapTickets.com >
Consolidator Networks	(888) 942-8258	< AirValues.com >
Council Travel (for students)	(800) 226-8624	< CouncilTravel.com >

Appendix F
Charter and Consolidator Resources

DER Travel Services	(800) 337-6593	< DERtravel.com >
D-FW Tours	(800) 527-2589	< DFWtours.com >
Discount Travel	(877) 359-0212	< DiscountTravelInt.com >
Discount Travel Center	(408) 238-9840	< WholesaleAirTravel.com >
Discount Travel Wholesalers		< DTravel.com>
Discover Wholesale Travel	(800) 576-7770	none
Funjet Vacation Pleasure Break	(800) 777-1566	< PleasureBreak.com >
Interworld	(800) 468-3796	< InterworldTravel.com >
Overseas Express	(800) 343-4873	< Ovex.com >
Safar International	(800) 544-2369	< SafarInt.com >
STA Travel (for students)	(800) 781-4040	< STAtravel.com >
TFI Tours International	(800) 745-8000	none
Ticket Planet, Inc.	(800) 799-8888	< TicketPlanet.com >
Travac	(800) 872-8800	< Travac.com >
Travel Network	(800) 933-5963	< Travel-Network.com >
UniTravel	(800) 325-2222	< UniTravel.com >
Whole Earth Travel Air Hitch	(888) 247-4482	< 4CheapAir.com >

Discount Travel Agencies (Rebaters)

Lowestfare.com	(888) 777-2222	< LowestFare.com >
Pennsylvania Travel	(877) 251-6866	< PaTravel.com >
Travel Associates	(800) 992-7388	< TravelAssociates.com >
Travel Avenue	(800) 333-3335	< TravelAvenue.com >
Travel Discounters	(408) 923-6324	< TravelDiscounters.com >
Travel Wholesalers Int'l	(800) 487-8944	< GoTWI.com/fares.htm >

Others

Air Awards	(888) 222-2260	< airawards.com >
Travel Management Services		< frequentflyerpoints.com >
Last Minute Travel	(800) 527-8646	

< LowerAirfares.com/charter >

< LowerAirfares.com/consol >

Appendix G
Internet Sources

A complete up-to-date list of Internet Web sites can be found at:
< LowerAirfares.com/travlist.html >

General Tips

< Air-fare.com >
< Airtravel.About.com >
< ArtOfTravel.com >
* < BestFares.com >
< DiscountAirfares.com >
< Frommers.com >
< JaxFax.com/links.html >
< LowerAirfares.com/tips.html >
< RulesoftheAir.com >
< SavvyTraveler.com >
< ShoestringTravel.com >
< TravelersNet.com >
< UndergroundTravel.com >

Booking Engines and Low Fare Finders

* < 1travel.com >
* < Expedia.com >
* < Flifo.com>
* < Gotwi.com/fares.htm >
* < Hotwire.com >
* < ITN.net >
* < QIXO.com >
* < TheTrip.com >
* < TISS.com >
* < TravelHub.com >
* < Travelocity.com >
* < Travelscape.com >

Web Sites with Airline Lists:

< AirlineData.com/airlines.htm >
< Airlines.com/directory.cfm >
< AirWebTravel.net/airlines >
< Chicago.com/air/carriers >
< FAA.gov/airlineinfo.htm >
< Flyaow.com/airlines.htm >
< ITN.net/airlines >
< Period.com/airlines >
< SmilinJack.com/airlines.htm >

Frequent Flyer

* < BizTravel.com >
< FlyerTalk.com >
< FrequentFlier.com >
< FrequentTraveler.com >
< WebFlyer.com >

Mailing Lists (Listservs)

< Liszt.com >

General Search Engines

< Google.com >
< NorthernLight.com >

Travel Search Engines

< Kasbah.com >
* < Travel.com >
< Traveling.com >

Newsgroups

< Deja.com > (lists all newsgroups)
alt.airline.schedules
alt.travel (and alt.travel.uk.air)
biz.listserv.airline
misc.transport.air-industry
rec.travel.% (%=.air, .misc, others)

* also has flight booking engines

Appendix G
Internet Sources

Last-Minute Airfares - E-Mail Notification Services

Air Canada	< AirCanada.ca >
Alaska Airlines	< AlaskaAir.com >
America West	< AmericaWest.com >
American Airlines	< AA.com >
Cathay Pacific	< Cathay-usa.com >
Continental Airlines	< Continental.com >
Icelandair	< Icelandair.com >
Northwest	< NWA.com >
Southwest Airlines	< Southwest.com >
TWA	< TWA.com >
United Airlines	< UAL.com >
US Airways	< USAirways.com >
Smarter Living	< SmarterLiving.com >

Travel Bookstores

California Map & Travel Center
Los Angeles, CA — < Mapper.com >

Distant Lands Travel Bookstore & Outfitters
Pasadena, CA — < DistantLands.com >

Globe Corner Bookstore
Cambridge, MA — < GlobeCorner.com >

The Literate Traveler
Beverly Hills, CA — < LiterateTraveler.com >

Phileas Fogg's Travel Center
Palo Alto, CA — < Foggs.com >

Powell's Travel Books
Portland, OR — < Powells.com >

Travel Books and Language Center
Washington, DC — < BookWeb.org/bookstore/travelbks >

The Travel Bug Bookstore
Vancouver, BC — < Swifty.com/tbug >

Traveler's Bookcase
Los Angeles, CA — < TravelBooks.com >

Wide World Books & Maps
Seattle, WA — < TravelBooksAndMaps.com >

The World Traveller Books & Maps
Chapel Hill, NC — < TravelBookshop.com >

Appendix H
Other Reading

General

Library: sections **910.2** and **917.3** include travel reference books. Check circulation AND Reference areas.

Bookstore: look for a **Travel-General** section that is separate from the destination guidebooks.

Ask a librarian or bookstore employee for assistance in finding a book or magazine for *any* subject.

Books

Air Courier Bargains. Monaghan, Kelly. The Intrepid Traveler.
The Air Courier's Handbook. Basye, Jennifer. Big City Books.
Airfare Secrets Exposed. Leach, Joel and Carey Christensen. Studio 4 Productions.
The Airline Passenger's Guerilla Handbook. Brown, George Albert. Blakes Publishing Group.
Bargain Travel Handbook. Hogsett, Suzanne. Travel Easy Publishing.
Cheap/Smart Travel. Fischer, Theodore. M. Evans and Company Inc.
Consumer Reports Best Travel Deals. Perkins, Ed. Consumers Union.
The Courier Air Travel Handbook. Field, Mark I. Perpetual Press.
Discount Airfares: The Insider's Guide, How to Save Up to 75% on Airline Tickets. Hobart, George E. Priceless Publications.
The Fearless Flyer. Hartman, Cherry. The Eighth Mountain Press.
Fly Cheap! Monaghan, Kelly. The Intrepid Traveler.
Fly Free, Stay Cheap! Mills, Vicki. Platypus Publications, Inc.
The Flying Smart Handbook. Horgan, Capt. (Ret.) Denis. FSH Publishing.
Frommer's What the Airlines Never Tell You. Clarke, Maureen. IDG Books Worldwide.
The Frugal Globetrotter. Northam, Bruce T. Fulcrum Publishing.
How to Fly Around the World Almost for Free As an Air Courier. Halken, William. Magni Co.
Insider Travel Secrets. Parsons, Tom. Best Fares USA, Inc.
Net Travel. Shapiro, Michael. Songline Guides and O'Reilly & Assoc., Inc.
Passport to Discounted Travel. Allen, Christopher. Worldview Press.
The Penny Pincher's Passport to Luxury Travel. Widzer, Joel L. Traveler's Tales Guides.
The Practical Nomad. Hasbrouck, Edward. Moon Travel.
The Safe Travel Book. Savage, Peter. Lexington Books.
The Savvy Adventure Traveler. Dudley, Ellen. Ragged Mountain Press.

Appendix H
Other Reading

10 Minute Guide to Travel Planning on the Net. Pack, Thomas. Que Corporation.

Tips for the Savvy Traveler. Burns, Deborah. Storey Publishing.

Travel Rights. Leocha, Charles. World Leisure Corp.

Travel Smarts. Teison, Herbert and Nancy Dunnan. The Globe Pequot Press.

Travel Tips for Teachers. Bloyd, Sunni. Lowell House.

The Traveler's Sourcebook. Smith, Darrin and Nancy Kniskern. Omnigraphics, Inc.

Traveling Smart. Uber, Carolyn Hayes. Dragonflyer Press.

Trouble-Free Travel. Colwell, Stephen D. and Ann R. Shulman. Nolo Press.

Unbelievably Good Deals and Great Adventures That You Absolutely Can't Get Unless You're Over 50. Heilman, Joan Rattner.

Unfair at Any Fare. Roberts, Lawton. Essence Publishing.

The Unofficial Business Traveler's Pocket Guide. McGinnis, Christopher J. McGraw-Hill.

The Virgin Student Travellers Handbook. Griffiths, Tom. Virgin Publishing Ltd.

The Worldwide Guide to Cheap Airfares. McColl, Michael Wm. Insider Publications.

You Can Travel Free. Kirk, Robert Wm. Pelican Publishing Company.

Magazines

Arthur Frommer's Budget Travel
(800) 829-9121
< Frommers.com >

Best Fares
(800) 880-1234
< BestFares.com >

Conde Nast Traveler
(800) 777-0700
< Epicurious.com/travel >

Consumer Reports Travel Letter
(800) 234-1970
< ConsumerReports.org >

Expedia Travels
(877) 388-7764
< eTravels.net >

Inside Flyer
(800) 209-2870
< WebFlyer.com >

International Travel News (ITN)
(800) 486-4968
< IntlTravelNews.com >

JaxFax
(203) 655-8746
< JaxFax.com >

National Geographic Traveler
(800) 647-5463
< NationalGeographic.com>

Travel & Leisure
(800) 888-8728
< TravelAndLeisure.com >

Travel Holiday
(303) 604-1464
< TravelHoliday.com >

Travelocity Magazine
(800) 365-7635
< TravelocityMag.com >

Figures

Web Sites

Following are Web sites listed in *Winning the Airfare Game,* except for the Appendices. Since Web site addresses can change at any time, an updated, current list of Web sites will be kept at < LowerAirfares.com/websites >.

Routes

Specific routes used in *Winning the Airfare Game* are listed here. In most cases, a specific route is used for illustrative purposes but the principle applies to many or all routes.

Index

A

B

C

D

E

F

G

H

I

J

K

L

M

N

O

T

U

Visit **HawkRidgePress.com** or **LowerAirfares.com** for current sales and specials along with additional ordering options—including using a credit card or submitting by telephone or fax.

ORDER FORM

Please send _____ copies of **Winning the Airfare Game** to:

Name: ______________________________
Address: ______________________________
City: ______________ State: _____ Zip: __________
Telephone: ______________ E-mail: ______________

Subtotal (# of books @ $13.95 each) _______
Shipping ($4 for first book, $2 for each additional book) _______
4.5% Sales Tax (for Virginia addresses only) _______
TOTAL _______

Send check or money order for TOTAL to:

Hawk Ridge Press
P. O. Box 2755
Reston, VA 20195-0755

ORDER FORM

Please send _____ copies of **Winning the Airfare Game** to:

Name: ______________________________
Address: ______________________________
City: ______________ State: _____ Zip: __________
Telephone: ______________ E-mail: ______________

Subtotal (# of books @ $13.95 each) _______
Shipping ($4 for first book, $2 for each additional book) _______
4.5% Sales Tax (for Virginia addresses only) _______
TOTAL _______

Send check or money order for TOTAL to:

Hawk Ridge Press
P. O. Box 2755
Reston, VA 20195-0755